# DECOLONISING LANGUAGE EDUCATION

Jaime Hoerricks

# DECOLONISING LANGUAGE EDUCATION

## Reframing English Language Development for Multilingual and Neurodiverse Learners

Education Studies

Collection Editor

Janise Hurtig

First published in 2025 by Lived Places Publishing



British Library Cataloguing in Publication Data
A CIP record for this book is available from the British Library.

ISBN: 9781917503938 (pbk)
ISBN: 9781917503952 (ePDF)
ISBN: 9781917503945 (ePUB)



Cover design by Fiachra McCarthy
Book design by Rachel Trolove of Twin Trail Design
Typeset by Newgen Publishing, UK

Lived Places Publishing
P.O. Box 1845
47 Echo Avenue
Miller Place, NY 11764

www.livedplacespublishing.com

# Abstract

*Decolonising Language Education* revolutionises the current approach to English Language Development (ELD), particularly for multilingual and neurodiverse learners, including those identified as Gestalt Language Processors (GLPs). In the context of primary and secondary school education, this book challenges the colonial mindset embedded within modern ELD practices, which prioritise English proficiency at the expense of home language development – an approach that reflects historical power dynamics rather than linguistic realities.

Drawing from the Natural Language Acquisition model and critical pedagogy, *Decolonising Language Education* advocates for a transformative methodology that acknowledges and values the diverse linguistic and neurological profiles of students. This includes a particular focus on neurodivergent learners, such as the estimated 75% who are GLPs, who are often misunderstood or unsupported in traditional language instruction settings.

The book equips educators with practical strategies, case studies, and classroom examples that promote inclusive and equitable learning environments. These environments honour the natural language acquisition processes of multilingual and neurodiverse students, fostering growth that embraces both home and target languages. Building upon the foundational work from Holistic Language Instruction (Hoerricks, 2024), this text applies these insights specifically to ELD and TESOL contexts.

Ultimately, *Decolonising Language Education* is a call to action for educators to dismantle colonial assumptions in language instruction, embrace culturally responsive practices, and bridge the gap between progressive educational initiatives and the realities of mainstream practice. By adopting this inclusive framework, educators can empower all learners to thrive within and beyond the classroom, ensuring that their linguistic identities are recognised and respected in the learning process.

## Key words

Decolonising education, english language development, gestalt language processing, analytic language processing, multilingual learners, neurodiverse education, critical pedagogy, natural language acquisition, inclusive practices, culturally responsive teaching, equitable language instruction, power threat meaning framework

# Contents

# Introduction

## Learning objectives

- Understand the colonial roots of current English Language Development practices and their detrimental effects on multilingual and neurodiverse learners, particularly Gestalt Language Processors.
- Recognise the importance of adopting a decolonised approach that not only uplifts and supports home languages alongside English but also empowers students through the integration of their cultural and linguistic identities.
- Be able to apply the principles of Natural Language Acquisition and critical pedagogy to design more inclusive and equitable language instruction.
- Use the Power Threat Meaning Framework to assess the social, cultural, and psychological impact of current ELD practices on marginalised students.
- Be able to design classroom practices that support diverse linguistic and neurological profiles, using a transformative educational methodology.

## Rationale

The purpose of this introduction is to lay the groundwork for understanding the historical and systemic issues embedded in current English Language Development (ELD) practices. These practices often prioritise English at the expense of home languages, reflecting a colonial legacy that marginalises both the linguistic and cultural identities of multilingual and neurodiverse learners. Recognising these colonial roots challenges educators to reconsider the conventional focus on English, inviting them to explore more inclusive alternatives.

The Power Threat Meaning Framework plays a crucial role in this rethinking, offering a lens to examine how power dynamics shape language instruction. Rather than viewing the challenges faced by multilingual students as individual deficits, the PTMF encourages educators to see these difficulties as responses to systemic pressures. This shift in perspective fosters a more inclusive and equitable approach, where home languages are not merely acknowledged but actively uplifted and supported, strengthening students' sense of identity and belonging.

Throughout the chapter, you will see how the Natural Language Acquisition model and critical pedagogy provide the foundation for a transformative educational approach that meets the needs of Gestalt Language Processors (GLPs) and other neurodiverse learners. (GLPs will be defined in detail later in the text.) This framework bridges theoretical foundations with practical applications in real-world educational settings, illustrating the need for systemic change.

As we explore these concepts, the introduction aims to connect the broader goals of decolonising language education with your everyday classroom experiences, equipping you to challenge entrenched practices and implement more equitable instruction. To support your engagement with the material, you may find it helpful to refer to the glossary of terms at the end of the book, especially as key concepts and acronyms are introduced throughout.

## Meet the author

For most of my life, I have been a foreigner – sometimes quite literally, as I've moved across countries and cultures, restarting my life in entirely new contexts. But more often, I've felt foreign in a less tangible way. As an autistic GLP, my relationship with language has always been complex (Hoerricks, 2023; Hoerricks 2024). The words others take for granted as tools of expression often feel distant, foreign objects that I must painstakingly learn, piece by piece, to function in the world.

Each time I had to restart my life in a new location, I was forced to learn the "language" of my new existence from scratch. Whether it was a literal language – English, Spanish, German – or the unwritten social rules of a new community, the process was slow, fragmented, and often frustrating. It always took time for me to get up to speed, and even then, I never felt fully "at home." There was always a part of me that remained foreign, out of place, forever a few steps behind the linguistic and cultural nuances of my new life.

This sense of being an outsider informs the way I see my students today – many of whom are multilingual and neurodiverse, grappling with an education system that, like my own experiences, assumes fluency where there is none. In California's ELD programs, the assumption is often that English is used not just in school but also at home and in students' social lives. But this is far from true. For most of my students, English is only spoken in the classroom. Everywhere else, their home language dominates – within their families, social circles, and communities. In this environment, how can we expect their English language skills to flourish when the world outside of school is closed off to the language we're trying to teach them?

My experience of feeling foreign in my own body and language has given me a unique lens to see the challenges multilingual and neurodiverse students face in language learning. It is not enough to simply teach a second language in the classroom if we ignore the social and cultural realities outside it. Language cannot grow in isolation. Like me, my students are often trapped between two worlds – one in which they must function academically in English, and another in which their home language provides their only real sense of belonging. The dissonance between these worlds can stunt their language growth and, more importantly, their confidence and identity as learners.

## My educational background

In my nearly six decades, my journey through education has been a series of resets, abrupt stops, and restarts. These shifts mark different acts in my life, each requiring me to learn new languages – both literally and figuratively – and often feeling foreign in each new context.

Act I of my life was defined by survival. Circumstances offered no handholds, and I navigated the world in a state of isolation and illiteracy, without the linguistic tools others took for granted. Act II continued this struggle, as I remained a functionally illiterate adult, relying on strength and instinct to move through life and the globe. My hands understood the physical language of strength and precision long before I could read or write. However, at the end of Act II, I finally gained literacy – a turning point that transformed my path. This newfound skill led to a chance social meeting that opened the door to a career in forensic science, once again resetting my language journey, as I had to learn the technical language and systems of a new professional field.

Act III saw me pursue formal education to solidify this career. I earned a bachelor's and master's degree in Organizational Leadership from Woodbury University, a Master of Education in Instructional Design from Western Governors University (WGU), and a PhD in Education from Trident University. These degrees reflect my work in forensic science, helping me navigate and master the professional systems of power I had entered.

Now in Act IV, I've transitioned into teaching, a field that demands continuous learning. I earned a Master of Education in Special Education from Loyola Marymount University, and I am currently pursuing a Master of Education in English Language Learners from WGU. At the same time, I am completing the induction process at Mt. St. Mary's University to clear my probation as a teacher and earn a lifetime teaching credential. Alongside this, I've earned various certifications, including a 150-hour TEFL certificate from the University of Toronto, a 40-hour Orton-Gillingham certification, and a 90-hour Early Literacy certificate from the Rollins Centre for Language and Literacy in Atlanta, Georgia.

These degrees and certifications are not marks of brilliance or autistic savant abilities but are reflective of the gatekeeping mechanisms within education. Each phase of my life required me to learn the language of new academic, professional, and cultural contexts. As an autistic GLP, learning these new languages has taken time, effort, and significant financial resources, reflecting how power and privilege are maintained in colonial systems of education.

Through my story, I aim to illustrate how language, education, and power intersect to limit opportunities for those outside the dominant framework, while also demonstrating the resilience required to navigate these systems. Elements of my own language learning journey will be woven throughout the coming chapters, serving as an exemplar to ground the theoretical discussions in real-life experiences. By sharing these personal insights, I hope to provide a lens through which educators can better understand the challenges faced by diverse learners and the urgent need for reforms that embrace and support them.

## Preparing to study

Before diving into the material, it's important to reflect on the current systems of language education and your own position within them. This book challenges many of the assumptions that underlie ELD programs and seeks to create a more inclusive, equitable approach to language instruction. As you prepare to engage with this text, it's essential to adopt a mindset that is open to questioning the status quo and ready to explore alternative frameworks.

Start by reflecting on your experiences with language, both as a learner and as an educator. Consider the following questions:

- How have you seen power dynamics play out in your language learning or teaching experiences?
- What role do home languages play in your classroom or learning environment? Are they valued or sidelined?
- How do you currently approach neurodiverse learners, such as those who may process language differently, including Gestalt Language Processors (GLPs)?

This book is grounded in the belief that language is not neutral – it is intertwined with culture, power, and identity. As you move through each chapter, you'll be asked to consider how colonial legacies shape the way we teach and learn language, and how we might work to decolonise these practices. Be prepared to engage with case studies, reflective activities, and practical strategies that will help you apply these concepts in your own context.

Take time to think about the home languages of the students you teach or the communities you engage with. Consider how uplifting and supporting those languages can lead to greater language proficiency, cultural pride, and student empowerment. By centering multilingualism and neurodiversity, this book offers a vision of language education that is both inclusive and transformative.

Approach this journey with the understanding that change is possible, but it requires an intentional shift in how we view language, learning, and identity. This book is not just about improving language instruction but about creating a more just, decolonised educational experience for all learners.

# The politics of language in education

At the heart of ELD lies a political reality: language instruction has long been shaped by power dynamics that reflect colonial legacies. In many educational systems, particularly those with colonial histories, the prioritisation of English over home languages is not simply a matter of pedagogical preference, but a reflection of entrenched power structures. This practice marginalises both linguistic and cultural identities, forcing multilingual and neurodiverse learners to conform to a dominant language that may not reflect their home or community.

These power dynamics shape how language is taught and whose languages are considered valuable. The current system often imposes English as the sole language of academic success, reinforcing inequalities by sidelining home languages, which play a critical role in identity formation and cognitive development. For many students – especially those identified as GLPs – this imposition creates a disconnect between the language of instruction and their lived experiences, making it harder for them to succeed academically while maintaining a sense of belonging to their cultural and linguistic heritage.

# Check for understanding

As you prepare to engage with the material, take a moment to reflect on the key ideas introduced. Think about how colonial legacies may have influenced language education in your context. Do you recognise power dynamics that privilege English over home languages? Consider how this affects both multilingual and neurodiverse learners in your classroom or learning environment.

Ask yourself:

- How might decolonising ELD practices change your approach to teaching?
- What challenges do GLPs face in your current language instruction methods?
- How can you begin to uplift and support home languages more effectively?

These reflections will help you identify areas for growth and change as you move forward. Be prepared to revisit these questions throughout the book as you deepen your understanding of inclusive and equitable language education.

## Some things that might trip you up

Here are some potential challenges that you might face when engaging with this text:

- **Cultural and contextual differences:** Learners from different countries and educational systems may have varying experiences with colonial legacies in language education. While the book focuses on the context of ELD, readers from non-colonial or non-English-dominant nations may struggle to relate to examples based in U.S. or Western practices. This can lead to confusion about how the concepts apply to their local contexts.

  o Tip: Actively reflect on how your own educational system handles language instruction and whether similar power dynamics are present, even if not in the same form.

- **Understanding neurodiversity, especially GLPs:** Concepts like Gestalt Language Processing may be unfamiliar to you, particularly if you do not have experience working with neurodiverse populations. You might find it difficult to conceptualise how these processing differences manifest in the classroom and why they require specific teaching strategies.
    - Tip: Don't worry. I provide clear, accessible definitions and real-world examples throughout the book to ensure you understand these neurodiverse perspectives.
- **Unfamiliarity with decolonial theory:** Decolonial theory may be new to many learners, particularly those from regions where colonialism's impacts on education are not widely discussed. Terms like decolonisation and critical pedagogy could be difficult for you to grasp, especially if you have not been exposed to critical social theories before.
    - Tip: I'll offer clear explanations of key terms and concepts, supplemented with case studies and practical examples that illustrate how decolonial frameworks work in educational settings.
- **Language barriers and terminology:** Given the global audience of this text, language can be a challenge, particularly if you are engaging with academic English. The specialised terminology used in discussing neurodiversity, language acquisition, and colonialism might require extra effort for non-native speakers to comprehend. Don't worry. I've got you covered.
    - Tip: There's a glossary of key terms and phrases at the end of the book. Additionally, I tend to use accessible language whenever possible to minimise misunderstandings.

- **Application of theories to local contexts:** While the book may provide strategies and recommendations based on a Western or U.S.-centric system, you might struggle to see how these strategies can be adapted for your own educational environment, where resources, policies, and linguistic priorities differ significantly.
  - Tip: I encourage you to reflect on how the principles of uplifting home languages and supporting neurodiverse learners can be translated into your local context, even if specific recommendations differ.
- **Resistance to challenging established norms:** If you have been trained within traditional educational models, you may find the challenge to the status quo unsettling or difficult to accept. Decolonising language education requires questioning long-held beliefs and practices, which can provoke resistance or defensiveness, particularly if you are unfamiliar with the concept of systemic bias.
  - Tip: Let's use open dialogue, reflection, and discussion about the discomfort that comes with change. After all, it is part of the learning process.

## What can we do about it?

To counter the political forces that shape language instruction, we must actively work to dismantle the colonial assumptions that prioritise dominant languages over home languages. This begins with recognising that language is not neutral – it carries social, cultural, and political significance. By using frameworks like the PTMF and Critical Theory, educators can challenge the power structures that marginalise multilingual and neurodiverse learners.

From a practical standpoint, this means creating classrooms where home languages are seen as assets, not obstacles. By designing lessons that value students' cultural and linguistic backgrounds, we can foster inclusive environments where language instruction supports both academic success and personal identity. Rather than enforcing a monolingual framework, we can encourage the use of home languages alongside English to build a more holistic approach to learning.

Moreover, educators can use the PTMF to shift their perspective on language difficulties. Instead of seeing multilingual learners as deficient, we can view their challenges as responses to systemic pressures, advocating for an educational model that uplifts their strengths rather than focusing on their perceived weaknesses.

## Summary

Welcome to *Decolonising Language Education*. As you embark on this journey, I invite you to step into a critical space where language, identity, and power intersect. Throughout this book, we will challenge many of the assumptions underlying ELD practices and explore how these systems, rooted in colonial history, continue to shape the lives of multilingual and neurodiverse learners – learners like the GLPs who are so often overlooked by traditional methods.

My own journey has been one of constant resets – a series of starts and stops that have forced me to relearn the language of new contexts, professions, and systems. Like many of the learners we'll discuss in this book, I've felt foreign in every new act of life. These experiences have shaped the way I view education: not as a one-size-fits-all structure, but as a living, breathing ecosystem that must be adapted to the diverse needs of its inhabitants.

This book asks you to reflect on your own experiences with language. How have power dynamics shaped the way you've learned or taught language? How have the home languages of your students or communities been valued – or sidelined? These are important questions because language isn't just about communication. It's about belonging, identity, and power – the power to express oneself fully or to feel silenced in a world that prioritises dominant languages.

Through the lens of the PTMF and Critical Theory, we will deconstruct the traditional approaches to language education. The PTMF allows us to shift away from seeing learners' struggles as deficits within themselves and instead to view them as responses to a system that was never designed with their strengths in mind. This perspective is particularly powerful for neurodiverse learners like GLPs, whose ways of processing language have often been misunderstood and unsupported. The task before us is to create inclusive environments that validate these learners' experiences and provide them with the tools they need to succeed – not by forcing them to conform to existing systems but by transforming those systems to meet their needs.

At the heart of this transformation is the social function of language. Language is not just a tool for academic achievement; it is a vital connector between individuals and their cultures, families, and communities. We will explore how uplifting home languages within the classroom context does more than improve language proficiency – it fosters pride, confidence, and a deep sense of belonging. This is a crucial step in decolonising education: recognising that bilingualism and multilingualism are not barriers to be overcome but strengths to be celebrated.

By embracing the ideas in this book, you are beginning a journey that will require you to question, reflect, and adapt. You'll be asked to reimagine your classrooms and teaching practices, not just as places where students learn English, but as spaces where equity and inclusion thrive. I won't claim this journey is easy – change never is – but I believe it is a necessary one. This is not only about improving language outcomes but about creating a more just and equitable educational system – one that honours the diversity of all learners.

So, I welcome you to this learning adventure with open arms. As you move through the pages ahead, think of this as an invitation to step outside the familiar, to reimagine what language education can be, and to take part in a broader movement towards decolonising education. I wish you bon voyage on this journey – may it be one of growth, discovery, and transformation. And most importantly, I wish you *bonne chance* – good luck in applying these ideas in your own context, as together we work towards a more inclusive, empowering approach to language education.

# 1 The colonial legacy of ELD: Language suppression and the need for dual development

## Learning objectives

1. Understand how ELD, rooted in TESOL frameworks, perpetuates assimilation rather than fostering bilingual development.
2. Recognise how a TEFL approach, acknowledging English as context-specific, better aligns with multilingual learners' realities.
3. Identify systemic barriers that prevent home language support and perpetuate inequity.
4. Introduce the necessity of a liberatory pedagogy that fosters simultaneous development of BICS and CALP in both home language and English.

## Rationale

The learning goals outlined in this chapter are grounded in a critical examination of the historical and ideological underpinnings of English Language Development programs, particularly those rooted in TESOL frameworks. These goals seek to disrupt the long-standing assumption that English proficiency must be achieved through linguistic assimilation, an approach that has its roots in colonial language suppression and continues to shape educational policy today. By reframing English instruction through a TEFL-informed lens and advocating for the simultaneous development of Basic Interpersonal Communication Skills and Cognitive Academic Language Proficiency in both English and students' home languages, this chapter positions bilingualism not as an obstacle but as a vital asset. The objectives also reflect an urgent need to challenge systemic barriers that marginalise linguistic diversity, including English-only policies that reinforce linguistic hierarchies and fail to accommodate the cognitive and cultural needs of multilingual and neurodiverse learners. As the chapter demonstrates, a liberatory pedagogy – one that affirms and integrates students' full linguistic repertoires – offers not only a more equitable model of language education but also a more effective pathway to academic success. These learning goals, therefore, are not merely theoretical but serve as essential guideposts for transforming ELD into a tool of empowerment rather than assimilation.

## Introduction: The paradox of ELD

ELD programs are built on the assumption that English should be central to students' lives beyond the classroom, a perspective deeply embedded in TESOL frameworks. These programs operate with the expectation that students will not only acquire English for academic purposes but will also integrate it into their broader social and personal identities. Burchell et al. (2024) highlight how this assimilationist ideology underpins many ELD policies, treating home languages as barriers to success rather than essential components of a student's linguistic repertoire. The result is an approach that implicitly, and sometimes explicitly, encourages the replacement of students' first languages with English, reinforcing cultural assimilation as an unspoken objective of language instruction.

Housel (2021) further critiques this monolingual focus, noting that many TESOL programs are designed with an assumption that students will transition to exclusive English use, often failing to acknowledge the continued role of home languages in students' lives. This perspective marginalises linguistic diversity and places undue pressure on multilingual learners to conform to an English-dominant framework that does not reflect their lived experiences. When English is framed as the primary and most valuable language, students' home languages are often viewed as secondary, irrelevant, or even detrimental to their academic success. Consequently, educational policies and classroom practices frequently devalue students' linguistic and cultural assets, contributing to linguistic insecurity and identity erosion.

In contrast, a TEFL-oriented perspective offers a fundamentally different approach to English instruction. Rather than assuming that English must become a student's dominant language, TEFL treats English as a contextual skill – one used primarily for academic and professional settings rather than as a replacement for a learner's home language. Kamhi-Stein et al. (2021) argue that this situational framing empowers learners to engage with English as a functional tool while maintaining their primary linguistic and cultural identities. Unlike TESOL, which often positions English as the end goal of language education, TEFL acknowledges the legitimacy of multilingualism and does not demand linguistic assimilation as a condition for academic success.

This distinction is particularly important when considering the role of schools in students' linguistic development. For many multilingual learners, English is not the dominant language in their home or community, making the expectation of full immersion unrealistic. Burchell et al. (2024) highlight that TESOL frameworks often disregard this reality, assuming that English acquisition should occur at the expense of home language maintenance. However, if schools were to adopt a TEFL-informed approach, they could reframe English as a supplementary skill rather than a replacement language. This shift would not only validate students' linguistic backgrounds but also foster a more inclusive learning environment where multilingualism is recognised as an asset rather than a deficiency.

Reframing ELD in this way challenges the deficit-based narratives that have long shaped language education policy. Instead of positioning English as the singular path to success, a contextual skill-based model acknowledges the rich linguistic knowledge that students bring into the classroom. Kamhi-Stein et al. (2021) emphasise that when educators take this approach, students are better able to engage with English in ways that are meaningful and relevant to their specific needs, rather than being pressured to abandon their home languages in favour of full assimilation. By recognising school as a 'foreign' linguistic space for many students, educators can create learning environments that support language development without enforcing linguistic conformity.

Ultimately, adopting a TEFL-inspired perspective in ELD programs allows students to engage with English as a valuable but context-specific tool, rather than as a replacement for their existing linguistic identities. This shift not only empowers multilingual learners but also challenges the systemic inequities that have long shaped English language instruction. By moving away from the assimilationist assumptions embedded in TESOL frameworks, educators can foster an approach that honours linguistic diversity while ensuring that students acquire the skills they need to navigate academic and professional spaces with confidence.

## Historical context: Colonial language policies and their legacy

Colonial powers have long wielded language as a tool of domination, enforcing linguistic hierarchies that privileged the colonisers' language while systematically erasing indigenous and minority languages. This process was not merely about linguistic replacement but about restructuring entire social systems to align with colonial governance. Colonial governments and missionary institutions understood that severing communities from their linguistic and cultural roots was essential to maintaining control over colonised populations. Jayasinghe (2021) examines how colonial-era education systems deliberately imposed the language of the colonisers, creating a generational disconnect between indigenous communities and their linguistic heritage.

This linguistic displacement was a means of eroding indigenous knowledge systems, enforcing new social hierarchies, and cementing colonial authority.

A particularly egregious example of this was the widespread use of Indigenous boarding schools, especially in North America and Australia. These institutions were designed to strip indigenous children of their languages, cultures, and identities by forcibly removing them from their homes and immersing them in English-only environments. Speaking their home languages was harshly punished, with children facing physical abuse, isolation, or public humiliation for any linguistic transgressions. The ideological foundation of these schools was clear: indigenous languages were seen as obstacles to 'civilisation,' and full assimilation into the dominant colonial culture was the expected outcome. These practices were not unique to North America; similar strategies were deployed in British and French colonial territories across Africa and South Asia, where the official languages of governance and education were imposed at the expense of local languages (Kazmi, 2022). The colonial project sought not only to control land and resources but also to control thought and identity – language was the primary means by which this was achieved.

Although overt coercion is no longer the standard mechanism of language suppression, the ideological foundations of these colonial policies persist in modern ELD programs, particularly those shaped by TESOL frameworks. The fundamental assumption remains unchanged: English is prioritised at the expense of home languages, reinforcing linguistic hierarchies and promoting assimilation under the guise of educational advancement. Kazmi

(2022) argues that contemporary TESOL practices continue to reflect a colonial legacy in which access to power and opportunity is framed as being contingent on English proficiency, rather than embracing a multilingual approach that validates linguistic diversity. While the explicit punishment of home language use may have diminished, the systemic devaluation of non-English languages persists through policies that fail to actively support multilingualism.

This marginalisation of home languages is not incidental – it is a direct extension of colonial ideologies that positioned English as the language of modernity, intelligence, and progress. Kaveh (2020) highlights how English-only policies in the United States, which restrict bilingual education and discourage the use of home languages in classrooms, stem from the same assimilationist frameworks that drove colonial education systems. These policies frame non-English languages as impediments to academic success rather than as vital cognitive and cultural resources. In many U.S. states, bilingual education is either severely restricted or absent altogether, forcing multilingual learners to navigate an education system that privileges English at the expense of their linguistic identities. This mirrors colonial practices where indigenous and local languages were systematically erased to elevate the language of the coloniser.

Despite extensive research demonstrating the benefits of bilingual and multilingual education, TESOL-based ELD programs continue to prioritise English monolingualism as the default measure of linguistic success. Instead of recognising multilingualism as an asset, many of these programs reinforce the idea that linguistic diversity is a problem to be 'fixed' rather than a strength to be nurtured. By doing so, they perpetuate deficit-based narratives that frame multilingual students as inherently disadvantaged rather than acknowledging the systemic barriers imposed on them.

Understanding this historical context is essential to moving beyond assimilationist models and towards an approach that genuinely respects and fosters linguistic diversity. The notion that English should be central to students' lives beyond school is not a neutral educational stance – it is a direct continuation of colonial linguistic policies. Recognising the parallels between historical language suppression and modern TESOL frameworks allows educators and policymakers to challenge the structural biases that continue to shape language education.

Reframing ELD through a decolonial lens requires dismantling the long-standing assumption that English proficiency must come at the expense of home language development. It means acknowledging that linguistic hierarchies are not natural or inevitable but are instead the result of deliberate policy decisions designed to uphold existing power structures. Kaveh (2020) emphasises that resisting these legacies involves actively creating educational spaces where home languages are not merely tolerated but celebrated as essential components of students' identities and academic success.

Thus, the persistence of colonial language ideologies in modern TESOL and ELD frameworks highlights the need for a fundamental shift in language education. Rather than replicating the assimilationist goals of colonial schooling, educators must advocate for models that position multilingualism as the norm rather than the exception. This requires systemic policy changes that support bilingual education, curriculum reforms that integrate students' linguistic backgrounds, and pedagogical approaches that challenge the entrenched belief that English should be the sole or dominant language of instruction. Only by addressing these colonial legacies can ELD truly serve the diverse linguistic needs of multilingual learners – without reinforcing the erasure and marginalisation that has defined language education for generations.

## Rethinking ELD goals: The TESOL vs TEFL divide

TESOL frameworks operate on the assumption that English should not only be the primary language of instruction but also the dominant language in students' lives beyond the classroom. This belief underpins many ELD programs, which implicitly position English as a necessary linguistic identity for academic, professional, and social success. Mason et al. (2024) critique this monolingual focus, arguing that TESOL disregards the linguistic realities of multilingual learners, who continue to use their home languages in family, community, and cultural contexts. Rather than recognising multilingualism as an asset, TESOL-based models often treat English as a replacement language rather than an additional tool, reinforcing the assimilationist ideologies that have long shaped language education policy.

This approach assumes that English must supersede home languages rather than coexist with them, a fallacy that has significant cognitive, social, and cultural consequences. When home languages are marginalised in education, students are often forced into a subtractive bilingualism model, where acquiring English proficiency comes at the direct expense of their first language. Tomaš et al. (2020) highlight that this model overlooks the cognitive and social benefits of bilingualism, instead treating non-English languages as obstacles to academic achievement. The expectation that students will use English in all aspects of life ignores the reality that for many, English is a situational necessity rather than a core part of their identity. By framing linguistic success in terms of full English immersion, TESOL reinforces a linguistic hierarchy that devalues home languages, leading to language erosion and cultural displacement.

In contrast, TEFL offers a fundamentally different approach, one that positions English as a situational skill rather than a dominant linguistic identity. Arnautović (2022) describes how TEFL equips learners with functional English proficiency for academic, professional, or travel-related contexts, while still maintaining the primacy of their home language. This model treats English as a supplementary tool, allowing students to engage with it as needed without pressuring them to abandon their linguistic and cultural backgrounds. Unlike TESOL, which assumes a long-term and full linguistic transition to English, TEFL acknowledges that learners may only require English in certain domains and does not demand full assimilation.

While TEFL offers a step away from TESOL's assimilationist foundations, it still conceptualises languages as separate systems rather than allowing for fluid interaction between them. This distinction is critical in reframing ELD programs. When English is treated as a functional skill rather than an imposed linguistic identity, students retain agency over their language use. They are not expected to suppress their home language to achieve proficiency in English. Instead, they are encouraged to develop both languages in ways that reflect their lived realities. This shift empowers students by validating their home language as central to their identity while equipping them with the tools to use English effectively in academic and professional settings.

## TEFL as a step towards translanguaging

Although TEFL presents a more inclusive model than TESOL, it still assumes languages operate in separate, bounded spaces rather than acknowledging how multilingual learners naturally use their full linguistic repertoire. Translanguaging extends beyond TEFL by recognising that students do not neatly switch between languages, but instead engage dynamically with all their linguistic resources to construct meaning. Mason et al. (2024) argue that TEFL's structured separation of languages still enforces rigid assessment frameworks, measuring students' abilities solely through English proficiency and disregarding their broader linguistic competencies. While TEFL does not demand assimilation, it fails to fully embrace the fluid, interdependent nature of multilingual learning.

A translanguaging-informed ELD model moves beyond both TESOL and TEFL by allowing students to seamlessly integrate English and their home language in academic spaces. This means rather than restricting students to one language at a time, educators create an environment where multilingual learners can draw on their full linguistic toolkit to engage with content. Translanguaging does not simply accommodate multilingualism – it actively affirms it as a natural and necessary part of learning.

## Shifting ELD from assimilation to empowerment

By adopting a TEFL perspective within ELD programs, educators can move away from the assimilationist goals embedded in TESOL and towards a more inclusive and equitable model of language instruction. However, to create truly transformative learning environments, ELD must go beyond TEFL and embrace translanguaging. This requires shifting educational policies to support multilingual learners in developing English as a functional skill, rather than as a forced linguistic transition. Schools must move beyond monolingual instructional models and instead implement curricula that integrate students' home languages as vital components of their cognitive and academic development.

As such, rethinking the TESOL vs. TEFL divide in ELD programs is about challenging long-standing assumptions about language learning and identity. The insistence that English must be central to students' lives beyond school is not a neutral pedagogical stance; it reflects linguistic hierarchies rooted in colonial history. TEFL represents an important shift away from assimilationist models, but it does not fully embrace the complex and fluid nature of multilingual learning. To create truly equitable ELD programs, educators must adopt translanguaging approaches that allow students to engage with all their linguistic resources freely. By treating English as a skill rather than a cultural imposition, educators can empower students to navigate multiple linguistic spaces without abandoning their home languages. In doing so, they foster an educational environment that truly values linguistic diversity and affirms students' identities as multilingual learners.

## The harm of ELD's English-only focus: Misunderstanding BICS and CALP

ELD programs that adhere to an English-only model often fail to address the complexities of language acquisition, particularly the distinction between Basic Interpersonal Communication Skills (BICS) and Cognitive Academic Language Proficiency (CALP). Developed by Cummins in the 1970s, this framework highlights the gap between conversational fluency and the deeper linguistic competencies required for academic success. BICS refers to surface-level, everyday communication – the ability to engage in casual interactions such as making small talk, following simple instructions, or responding to greetings. These skills typically develop within one to two years of English exposure, leading to the misconception that students who appear fluent in social contexts are fully proficient in the language. However, CALP refers to the academic language required for engaging with complex texts, constructing arguments, and conducting critical analysis, which takes significantly longer – often five to seven years – to develop, even in ideal conditions. Guo & Feng (2024) highlight that without explicit support for CALP, multilingual learners struggle to meaningfully engage with academic content, regardless of their conversational fluency.

A critical factor in successful CALP development is the maintenance of home language proficiency. Research consistently shows that literacy skills in a student's first language provide the cognitive and linguistic foundation necessary for academic English acquisition. When students have a strong grasp of their home language, they can transfer conceptual knowledge, grammatical structures, and problem-solving strategies to English, enhancing their comprehension and analytical skills. Robertson & Graven (2020) illustrate how sidelining home languages disrupts this transfer process, leaving students with fragmented linguistic resources that undermine their long-term academic success. In South African classrooms, for example, students required to learn in English without home language support exhibited lower comprehension levels and struggled with subject-specific terminology, whereas those who received bilingual instruction demonstrated higher retention and engagement. These findings reinforce the idea that home language maintenance is not an obstacle to English acquisition but a crucial component of it.

Despite this overwhelming evidence, TESOL-based ELD programs continue to neglect the role of home languages in academic development, prioritising an immersion approach that assumes English proficiency must be achieved in isolation. This assumption is deeply flawed, as it disregards students' existing linguistic knowledge and forces them to construct academic competencies from scratch. Li (2021) critiques this approach, arguing that TESOL's monolingual bias creates an artificial learning environment, expecting students to learn complex academic concepts in a language they have not yet mastered. The result is a cycle of academic failure, where multilingual learners underperform not because of cognitive deficiencies, but because they are denied access to their full linguistic toolkit.

By enforcing an English-only model, ELD programs further isolate English from students' lived linguistic realities. Many multilingual learners continue using their home languages at home and in their communities, meaning that English remains an academic necessity rather than an all-encompassing linguistic identity. When schools enforce English-only policies, they create a disconnect between classroom learning and real-world communication, depriving students of essential scaffolding mechanisms. Zano & Baloyi (2019) argue that this artificial divide disadvantages multilingual learners by invalidating their linguistic knowledge and preventing them from using their home languages to enhance their English development. Instead of supporting learning, English-only policies alienate students and reinforce linguistic hierarchies that position English as inherently superior while devaluing other languages.

## A more effective alternative: Translanguaging

A more equitable and effective alternative to the English-only model is translanguaging, a pedagogical approach that encourages students to use their full linguistic repertoire throughout the learning process. Rather than treating languages as separate entities, translanguaging allows students to fluidly integrate both English and their home languages to enhance comprehension, expression, and critical thinking. Li (2021) highlights that translanguaging strategies, such as discussing complex ideas in one's home language before translating them into English, significantly improve academic engagement and outcomes. When students are allowed to think and process in their strongest language first, they develop a deeper understanding of academic content, which in turn enables them to express ideas in English with greater clarity and accuracy.

Additionally, translanguaging fosters a more inclusive and empowering classroom environment. Zano & Baloyi (2024) demonstrate that when students are encouraged to use their home languages as learning tools, they experience greater confidence, higher participation, and a stronger sense of belonging in academic spaces. This shift is particularly important for students from marginalised linguistic backgrounds, who often face systemic barriers to full educational access. By integrating translanguaging practices into ELD programs, educators can disrupt the harmful effects of monolingual instruction and create a learning environment where multilingual students thrive rather than struggle.

As such, English-only ELD programs misinterpret the process of language acquisition, assuming that BICS is a sufficient indicator of academic proficiency while neglecting the extensive support required for CALP development. The failure to integrate home language support stunts students' ability to engage meaningfully with academic content, placing them at a structural disadvantage. Research from Guo & Feng (2024) and Robertson & Graven (2020) highlights the detrimental effects of monolingual instruction, while Li (2021) and Zano & Baloyi (2024) provide compelling evidence for translanguaging as a more effective alternative. Moving beyond the assimilationist goals of traditional TESOL frameworks requires a fundamental shift in how ELD programs are designed. By embracing multilingual pedagogies that recognise and utilise students' linguistic resources, educators can foster academic success without demanding linguistic conformity. This is not merely a policy shift – it is an ethical imperative to create equitable learning environments that support, rather than suppress, linguistic diversity.

## Linguistic suppression in today's classrooms

School language policies frequently operate under an English-only mandate, enforcing the belief that students must exclusively use English in academic settings. While these policies are often framed as measures to enhance English proficiency, they function as mechanisms of linguistic suppression, discouraging students from using their home languages even when doing so would support comprehension and learning. Kani & İğsen (2022) argue that such policies are not neutral; they actively penalise multilingual students by creating an environment in which their linguistic identities are marginalised. When home languages are restricted, students experience a form of cultural erasure, receiving the implicit message that their linguistic backgrounds are incompatible with academic success.

### The psychological and academic toll of English-only policies

The consequences of these restrictive policies extend far beyond language use. Paterson (2020) highlights that multilingual students in English-only classrooms frequently report heightened anxiety, diminished confidence, and a weakened sense of belonging. When students are reprimanded or stigmatised for speaking their home languages, many begin to self-censor, even in informal peer interactions. This suppression fosters long-term disengagement, leading students to internalise the idea that their linguistic knowledge is unwelcome in academic spaces. Instead of creating an inclusive learning environment, English-only policies establish linguistic hierarchies, positioning English as the sole marker of academic legitimacy while devaluing students' existing linguistic skills.

Beyond these psychological effects, English-only instruction has measurable academic consequences. When students are prohibited from using their home languages to process complex ideas, they lose essential cognitive tools for comprehension and analysis. Research consistently shows that multilingual learners perform better academically when allowed to use their full linguistic repertoire, particularly in subjects requiring deep conceptual understanding (Kani & İğsen, 2022). By contrast, English-only classrooms create artificial barriers to knowledge acquisition, forcing students to grapple with new material in a language they have not yet mastered rather than allowing them to leverage their strongest linguistic skills. This approach slows content comprehension, deepens achievement gaps, and places students from marginalised linguistic communities at a severe disadvantage.

## The impact on neurodiverse learners, particularly Gestalt Language Processors

These restrictive policies are especially harmful to neurodiverse learners, particularly Gestalt Language Processors (GLPs), whose language development does not follow the standard analytic processing model. TESOL-based ELD programs, which assume a linear and structured path to English proficiency, fail to accommodate the needs of GLPs, whose learning is inherently multi-contextual and reliant on exposure to diverse linguistic inputs. Yang & Jang (2020) emphasise that GLPs benefit from multi-language environments, where they can process language holistically, often retaining and using larger language chunks before developing rule-based grammar structures. When confined to English-only instruction, these learners are denied access to the linguistic variety essential for their cognitive processing style, making it significantly harder for them to develop both BICS (social language) and CALP (academic language) effectively.

TESOL models generally fail to recognise that not all students engage with language in the same way. Yang & Jang (2020) critique these models for their rigid adherence to sequential language acquisition strategies, which assume that all learners move through the same linguistic stages at a uniform pace. This framework is particularly detrimental to GLPs, who require exposure to multiple linguistic contexts and benefit from the ability to engage with home languages alongside English. The insistence on monolingual instruction forces these students into an unnatural learning process, which does not align with their cognitive strengths, leading to frustration, disengagement, and, in many cases, withdrawal from language learning altogether.

## A more equitable approach: Embracing multilingual and neurodiverse pedagogies

Reforming ELD programs to better support both multilingual and neurodiverse learners requires a fundamental departure from the restrictive English-only mindset. Instead of enforcing linguistic conformity, schools should adopt policies that embrace translanguaging, allowing students to draw on their full linguistic resources to aid comprehension and engagement. This shift would not only support academic achievement but also foster a more inclusive educational environment, where linguistic diversity is recognised as a strength rather than a deficit. Paterson (2020) argues that classrooms that validate students' home languages create spaces where learners feel more confident and willing to participate, leading to better academic outcomes for all students, including those with neurodiverse processing styles.

Thus, English-only policies serve as a continuation of linguistic suppression under the guise of educational standardisation. These policies ignore extensive research demonstrating that multilingualism enhances cognitive flexibility, supports deeper learning, and strengthens students' overall linguistic competence. Moreover, they fail to account for the needs of neurodiverse learners, particularly GLPs, who require multi-language environments to develop effective communication strategies. Kani & İğsen (2022) and Paterson (2020) illustrate the psychological harm these policies inflict on students, while Yang & Jang (2020) highlight the specific barriers they create for neurodiverse learners. Moving beyond these outdated models requires a fundamental shift in how language education is conceptualised – one that recognises multilingualism and neurodiversity not as challenges to be overcome, but as essential components of an equitable and effective learning environment.

## The liberatory alternative: Dual language development as a human right

A truly equitable approach to ELD must move beyond monolingual, assimilationist frameworks that have long dominated language instruction. A TEFL-inspired, contextual framework provides a liberatory alternative – one that positions English as a situational tool rather than an identity-altering force. When schools are understood as 'foreign' linguistic spaces for many students, English instruction can be reframed as a functional skill for academic and professional navigation rather than as a replacement for students' home languages. This shift challenges the entrenched belief that linguistic success requires full English immersion, instead affirming bilingualism as the natural and most effective path to language proficiency.

### The evidence for dual-language education

Research overwhelmingly supports the benefits of dual-language education, demonstrating that bilingual learners achieve stronger academic outcomes than their monolingual peers. Johnson (2024) highlights that students in dual-language programs develop literacy in both languages simultaneously, which enhances academic performance across disciplines, not just in language-related subjects. He et al. (2021) further demonstrate that bilingual education strengthens cognitive flexibility, metalinguistic awareness, and problem-solving skills – critical advantages that monolingual approaches to ELD fail to cultivate. The assumption that English-only instruction accelerates proficiency is a misconception; in reality, true bilingual development leads to deeper comprehension, stronger academic performance, and greater long-term linguistic stability.

Beyond these academic benefits, validating home languages is crucial for student identity, resilience, and cultural pride. Ryan (2021) emphasises that when students see their home languages affirmed in the classroom, their confidence increases, and they are more likely to engage actively in learning. This is particularly critical for students from marginalised linguistic backgrounds, who often experience systemic pressure to abandon their linguistic heritage in favour of English. Dual-language education counteracts this erasure by positioning home languages as assets rather than barriers, reinforcing students' sense of belonging both within and beyond the school environment.

## Implementing a liberatory pedagogy in ELD

Educators play a key role in transforming ELD from a tool of assimilation into a model of empowerment. Domke et al. (2024) outline practical steps for shifting language education towards a dual-language approach, including:

- Designing curricula that incorporate students' linguistic and cultural knowledge
- Allowing multilingual expression in classroom discussions
- Using translanguaging strategies to support comprehension and engagement

By integrating culturally responsive teaching practices into ELD instruction, teachers can create classrooms where multilingual learners feel valued rather than marginalised. This approach fosters an academic environment where students thrive without having to sacrifice their linguistic identities.

## Language education as a human right

Shifting towards a dual-language model is not just pedagogically sound – it is an issue of justice. The insistence on English monolingualism in education is not only ineffective but also exclusionary, reinforcing linguistic hierarchies that privilege English while devaluing other languages. Johnson (2024) and He et al. (2021) demonstrate that bilingualism strengthens academic success, while Ryan (2021) and Domke et al. (2024) highlight how culturally affirming pedagogy fosters student empowerment.

True language education must uplift rather than suppress. Ensuring that multilingual learners develop proficiency in English without being forced to relinquish the languages that shape their identities is not only the most effective approach but also the most ethical.

# Looking ahead

As we move forward in rethinking ELD, it is essential to pause for critical self-reflection. Many educators, often unconsciously, operate under the assumption that students will – or should – use English as their primary language beyond the classroom. This belief, deeply embedded in TESOL frameworks, shapes teaching practices in ways that may not align with students' linguistic realities. Consider how this assumption influences your own approach to language instruction. Do you expect students to rely on English outside of school? How do your classroom policies reflect or challenge the idea that English should be central to their lives?

A TEFL-inspired perspective offers a powerful alternative, one that treats English as a situational skill rather than an identity-defining necessity. Reflect on how shifting towards this model could change your practice. Could you integrate students' home languages into instruction more intentionally? How might translanguaging strategies support comprehension and engagement? What would it look like to teach English not as a replacement language, but as a tool for academic and professional success while affirming students' existing linguistic identities? These questions invite a deeper awareness of the implicit biases that shape language education and offer a path towards more equitable, student-centered teaching.

This reflection leads naturally into the next chapter, which explores the profound identity-based consequences of assimilationist ELD practices. When students are pressured to abandon their home languages in favour of English, the impact extends beyond academics – it affects their sense of self, cultural connection, and belonging. Chapter 2 will examine how language and identity are intertwined, highlighting the ways in which ELD programs often force students into a linguistic and cultural divide. By understanding these dynamics, we can move towards an approach that not only fosters English proficiency but also affirms and uplifts students' full linguistic and cultural selves.

## Summary

This chapter has explored how ELD, when rooted in TESOL frameworks, often functions as a tool of assimilation, echoing colonial practices that marginalise home languages and reinforce linguistic hierarchies. By contrasting TESOL with TEFL, and introducing translanguaging as a more inclusive approach, we have examined how English can be reframed as a context-specific skill rather than a replacement for students' linguistic identities. Recognising the historical and systemic barriers that prevent dual-language development is essential for creating equitable learning environments. Multilingual learners thrive when their home languages are valued and integrated into instruction, and when BICS and CALP are developed in both English and their first language. This shift from assimilation to empowerment is not only pedagogically sound but also a matter of educational justice.

## Key takeaways

- TESOL-based ELD programs prioritise assimilation, often marginalising home languages and reinforcing colonial language hierarchies.
- TEFL offers a more equitable framework, treating English as a functional skill for academic and professional use, rather than a replacement for students' linguistic identities.
- Translanguaging empowers multilingual learners, allowing them to use their full linguistic repertoire to access academic content and express complex ideas.
- BICS and CALP must be developed in both English and home languages to ensure meaningful academic engagement and long-term success.
- Neurodiverse learners, especially Gestalt Language Processors (GLPs), require flexible, multilingual approaches that accommodate diverse language processing styles.
- Language education is a human rights issue – affirming home languages and fostering bilingual development is essential for educational equity and student empowerment.

By rethinking ELD through a decolonial and inclusive lens, educators can move beyond assimilationist models and create spaces where linguistic diversity is not only respected but celebrated. The next chapter will build on these insights by examining how language suppression impacts student identity and exploring the critical role of home language in fostering a sense of belonging and academic success.

# 2 The impact of ELD on home language and identity

## Learning objectives

1. Understand the relationship between home language and identity formation.
2. Recognise how ELD practices that prioritise English can erode cultural and linguistic identities.
3. Examine case studies illustrating the tensions multilingual learners face in navigating their home and school languages.
4. Explore practical strategies to support and integrate home languages into the classroom.

## Rationale

In multilingual classrooms, language is not simply a tool for instruction – it is a vessel of identity, culture, and belonging. Yet, educational systems that prioritise English often disregard the profound impact of home language on student well-being, familial relationships, and academic engagement. This chapter addresses the urgent need to reframe ELD through an equity lens, recognising that the suppression of home languages can lead to cultural disconnection, identity struggles, and diminished learning outcomes. By exploring the intersection of language, identity, and power, this chapter equips educators with the knowledge and strategies to support linguistic diversity, honour students' cultural heritage, and foster inclusive learning environments where all students can thrive without sacrificing vital parts of who they are.

## Introduction: Language as identity

### The role of home language

Language is more than a means of communication; it is a cornerstone of identity, shaping how individuals understand themselves and their place in the world. Home language carries familial, cultural, and historical significance, acting as a bridge between generations and a repository of collective memory (Nikitorowicz, 2012). For many multilingual learners, their first language is not merely a tool for expression but a vital link to their heritage, traditions, and sense of belonging.

Within families, home language fosters intergenerational communication, allowing children to connect with elders who may not speak English fluently. Schecter and Bayley (1997) found that multilingual children often serve as cultural mediators between school and home, navigating distinct linguistic and cultural expectations. When children retain proficiency in their home language, they are more likely to maintain strong familial bonds, as language is deeply tied to expressions of love, respect, and shared history. Conversely, language loss can create emotional distance between generations, leading to cultural alienation and fractured family relationships (Rovira, 2008).

Beyond the family unit, home languages are crucial for fostering cultural pride and resilience. Research by Lam and Catto (2023) highlights that heritage language speakers who actively use their home language report stronger connections to their cultural identities and exhibit higher levels of psychological well-being. In multilingual societies, these languages serve as markers of community belonging, reinforcing collective identity and shared experiences. For example, children who grow up in immigrant households often feel most at home when they engage with their linguistic heritage, finding comfort in the familiar sounds, idioms, and narratives embedded in their first language.

However, when education systems prioritise English at the expense of home languages, this fundamental aspect of identity is placed under threat. Mainstream ELD programs often fail to recognise the role of home languages in shaping students' identities, treating them as obstacles rather than assets. This erasure of linguistic heritage creates an environment where multilingual students must navigate between two worlds – the linguistic expectations of school and the lived reality of their home life.

## The impact of language suppression

Throughout history, language suppression has been used as a tool of cultural and political control, reinforcing linguistic hierarchies that privilege dominant languages while marginalising others. Colonial regimes, for example, systematically imposed their languages on Indigenous and colonised peoples, eradicating native tongues in favour of English, French, or Spanish (Rovira, 2008). In North America, Indigenous boarding schools actively prohibited Native American students from speaking their languages, punishing those who resisted and forcing generations into linguistic assimilation. These policies sought to sever indigenous communities from their cultural heritage, reinforcing the idea that their languages – and by extension, their identities – were inferior.

This legacy of linguistic erasure continues in contemporary education systems, where English-only policies dominate many ELD frameworks. Schecter and Bayley (1997), in their study of Mexican immigrant families in the United States, observed that children often felt institutional pressure to prioritise English for academic success. This dynamic risked reinforcing a deficit perspective in which bilingualism was implicitly treated as a hindrance rather than an asset. The consequences of such policies are profound: when students are forced to suppress their first language, they often experience feelings of shame, insecurity, and cultural disconnection (Lam & Catto, 2023). Many come to associate their home language with being "less educated" or "less capable," leading to internalised linguistic oppression – a phenomenon where individuals devalue their own linguistic heritage in favour of the dominant language.

Moreover, linguistic suppression can negatively impact academic performance and self-perception. Research suggests that students who are discouraged from using their home language struggle with cognitive flexibility and metalinguistic awareness, both of which are essential for higher-order thinking and academic success (Nikitorowicz, 2012). When students are unable to engage with content in their strongest language, their critical thinking skills, comprehension, and confidence suffer, ultimately widening educational disparities.

The intersection of language, identity, and power is central to understanding why ELD programs must move beyond assimilationist frameworks, which prioritise English at the expense of students' home languages and cultural identities, and instead adopt models that actively honour and sustain linguistic diversity. Recognising home language as an essential component of identity, rather than a barrier to academic achievement, is key to fostering inclusive educational environments.

### Looking ahead

This chapter will explore how English-dominant educational models contribute to an identity crisis among multilingual learners, examining the tension between home language retention and the pressure to conform to monolingual expectations. By analyzing case studies and empirical research, we will illustrate the real-world consequences of language suppression and advocate for home language integration as a critical tool for student success and well-being.

## The identity crisis in ELD

Following the discussion of language as a core part of identity, it is necessary to examine how ELD programs frequently force multilingual learners into an impossible position – one where they are expected to prioritise English at the expense of their home languages. This pressure to assimilate does not merely shape language use; it fundamentally alters students' relationships with their families and communities, and with their sense of self. The result is an identity crisis, in which students must navigate competing expectations from school and home, often at great psychological and academic cost.

## The pressure to assimilate

At the heart of the identity crisis in ELD is the unspoken expectation that English should replace a student's home language. Many ELD programs are rooted in the assumption that full English immersion is the most effective path to academic success, reinforcing the idea that bilingualism is a transitional stage rather than a long-term strength (Joubert & Sibanda, 2022). While these programs claim to support multilingual students, they often create an identity divide by devaluing the languages that form the foundation of students' cultural and familial lives.

This tension is particularly evident in schools where English-only models dominate instructional policy. Students internalise the message that their home language is not welcome in academic spaces, leading many to suppress it, even outside of school. O'Connor et al. (2018) found that students from immigrant backgrounds often experience a gradual erosion of their home language proficiency, especially when schools fail to integrate bilingual support. This erosion is not just linguistic; it severs an essential connection to family traditions, cultural knowledge, and intergenerational communication.

For many multilingual learners, this forced divide creates deep psychological distress. A middle school student interviewed in Serafini, Rozell, and Winsler's (2020) study described the experience of speaking Spanish at home but being reprimanded for using it at school:

> "My mom always tells me to practice Spanish, but I don't want to anymore. My teacher says English is more important. When I go home, I feel weird because my words don't come out right in Spanish. My family laughs, and I get mad. But at school, I can't use Spanish either, so I don't feel like I belong anywhere."

This experience of linguistic alienation – feeling disconnected from both school and home – illustrates the emotional toll of language suppression. Instead of fostering a sense of pride in bilingualism, many ELD programs inadvertently push students towards shame and insecurity, making them feel that fluency in English is the only path to acceptance.

Another layer of this identity divide emerges in the way students experience linguistic policing. In many classrooms, multilingual learners are discouraged – even punished – for using their home language, reinforcing a hierarchy where English is seen as the only legitimate language of success (Nurshatayeva & Page, 2019). Over time, students internalise this belief, leading some to actively reject their home language to avoid discrimination. This rejection often manifests as discomfort speaking their first language in public, embarrassment when interacting with family members who do not speak English fluently, or even resentment towards their cultural background.

## The cost of marginalising home languages

The consequences of home language suppression extend beyond identity struggles – they also have measurable academic and psychological effects. Research indicates that students who are forced to abandon their first language often experience a decline in overall academic performance. O'Connor et al. (2018)

found that bilingual students who maintained proficiency in their home language exhibited stronger cognitive and literacy skills than those who lost it. This aligns with broader research on bilingual advantage theory, which demonstrates that maintaining a home language supports metalinguistic awareness, problem-solving skills, and long-term academic success.

However, when students are expected to function exclusively in English, their cognitive load increases, as they are forced to learn complex academic concepts in a language they have not yet mastered. This puts them at an inherent disadvantage compared to native English speakers, leading to lower confidence, academic disengagement, and higher dropout rates in extreme cases (Serafini, Rozell, & Winsler, 2020).

Beyond academics, the psychological cost of language suppression is severe. Many students experience feelings of inadequacy, isolation, and cultural dissonance when their home language is devalued. The erosion of home language skills can create emotional distance between students and their families, as they lose the ability to communicate effectively with parents, grandparents, and extended relatives. For many immigrant families, maintaining a home language is crucial for passing down cultural traditions and values. When children lose this linguistic connection, it can lead to a breakdown in family relationships and a deepened sense of alienation. At the same time, it's important to recognise that some families – facing societal pressures and internalised narratives of success tied to English – may actively or passively encourage this linguistic shift, viewing English as a pathway to upward mobility or relying on their children as language brokers in English-dominant institutions. These dynamics highlight not only the role of schools as agents of State hegemony but also the broader assimilationist ideologies that immigrant families are often compelled to navigate.

For students who continue to struggle with English acquisition, the pressure to assimilate can cause lasting damage to self-esteem. Many develop imposter syndrome, feeling that they will never be "good enough" in either language. Some avoid speaking altogether, fearful of being ridiculed for their accents or grammatical errors. This linguistic insecurity can persist into adulthood, shaping career choices, social interactions, and overall confidence levels (Joubert & Sibanda, 2022).

## Reframing ELD to support identity

The crisis of linguistic identity loss in ELD is not an inevitable outcome – it is a policy choice that can be undone. Instead of reinforcing English dominance, language programs should recognise bilingualism as an asset, not a liability. Research overwhelmingly supports dual-language education models, which allow students to develop both their home language and English simultaneously, leading to higher academic achievement, stronger cultural pride, and reduced identity struggles (Nurshatayeva & Page, 2019). While implementation remains uneven, it is worth noting that some districts across the United States have adopted dual-language models with encouraging results – demonstrating that more inclusive language education is both possible and effective.

By acknowledging that students thrive when their full linguistic identities are valued, schools can move beyond outdated assimilationist policies towards more inclusive approaches that embrace linguistic and cultural diversity. The next section will further explore this shift by presenting case studies of students navigating the language divide, highlighting the challenges and successes of multilingual education models.

## Case studies: Navigating the language divide

The previous section outlined how ELD programs often force multilingual learners into an identity crisis, where their home language is marginalised, creating tensions between school and cultural belonging. To better understand these challenges, this section presents three case studies that illustrate how language policies impact identity formation, family relationships, and academic success.

These case studies highlight the experiences of a neurodiverse student, a family struggling with cultural disconnection, and students in bilingual programs, offering insights into the real-world consequences of language suppression and the potential benefits of multilingual education.

### Case study 1: A neurodiverse student balancing home language and English in an English-only classroom

Felipe is an eight-year-old Gestalt Language Processor (GLP) who speaks Spanish at home but attends an English-only classroom. Like many GLPs, Felipe acquires language in chunks – memorised phrases or full utterances – rather than through isolated vocabulary or grammatical rules. This means he relies on familiar scripts and echolalia, the repetition of previously heard phrases, to make meaning and communicate (Howard, Katsos, & Gibson,

2020). These scripts are not random; they often carry emotional or contextual significance and serve as building blocks for more flexible language over time. At home, Felipe thrives in a bilingual environment where Spanish provides the scaffolding for expressive and receptive language. However, in his English-only classroom, his gestalt processing style is not understood or supported. Instruction is focused on isolated phonics and vocabulary drills – approaches that assume analytic language development and do not accommodate his holistic processing needs. This mismatch between his natural language development and the instructional environment places Felipe at a disadvantage – not because he is incapable, but because the system fails to meet him where he is linguistically and neurologically. His experience underscores the compounded challenge faced by multilingual GLPs in monolingual, assimilationist classrooms: they are not only denied access to their home language but also to methods of instruction aligned with how they naturally acquire language.

At home, Felipe thrives in a bilingual environment, where he comfortably expresses himself using memorised phrases in Spanish. However, at school, his language processing style is misunderstood. Teachers expect him to learn English through isolated vocabulary and phonics-based instruction, which does not align with his gestalt processing needs. He struggles to adapt, often repeating long, memorised English phrases without fully understanding their grammatical structure.

As a result, Felipe faces dual challenges:

1. His neurodivergent communication style is not accommodated, leaving him without the support he needs to develop English meaningfully.

2. His home language is treated as a barrier rather than a resource, limiting his ability to use his stronger Spanish skills to scaffold English learning.

Because of this linguistic and cognitive mismatch, Felipe experiences frustration, disengagement, and a growing reluctance to participate in class discussions. His parents report that he is becoming quieter at home, speaking less in both Spanish and English – a sign that language suppression is not just failing him academically but also contributing to social withdrawal.

Felipe's experience highlights the urgent need for more inclusive and responsive ELD practices, particularly for neurodivergent students whose language development does not follow linear or analytic models. As a multilingual GLP, Felipe would benefit significantly from translanguaging strategies – pedagogical approaches that allow students to draw on all their linguistic resources, including their home language, to construct and express meaning. In fact, a growing body of research suggests that translanguaging is not only beneficial but a natural process for bilingual learners more broadly, reflecting how language is used dynamically in real-life communication. For GLPs in particular, who often rely on holistic, emotionally contextualised language processing, the ability to access both languages freely can be especially critical. If Felipe's teachers were to incorporate bilingual supports – such as previewing material in Spanish, allowing him to reflect in his home language before responding in English, or validating the use of familiar Spanish scripts – they could reduce cognitive overload and support more authentic communication. Such practices not only scaffold academic development but also strengthen emotional regulation, self-esteem, and a sense of belonging. Rather than viewing Spanish as a barrier, these approaches recognise it as an essential bridge to deeper engagement and language growth in both tongues.

### Reflection: On recognising patterns

Reading Felipe's story, I think about a student I once supported – a quiet, perceptive child who also spoke in scripts no one else understood. His language wasn't broken. It was precise, lyrical, emotionally exacting. But the curriculum moved too fast. The system translated his echolalia into failure. I still wonder who he might have become, had his way of communicating been seen as language, not as delay.

## Case study 2: A family's struggle with a child's loss of cultural connection due to ELD

Miriam and Daniel are parents of a six-year-old daughter, Sofia, who is in her first year of school. In their home, Spanish is the primary language, and they have made conscious efforts to preserve their cultural heritage by teaching Sofia about Mexican traditions, music, and family history.

However, after six months in an English-only kindergarten program, Sofia begins to refuse to speak Spanish at home. She insists that "English is better" and expresses frustration when her parents try to communicate with her in Spanish. Miriam notices that Sofia's Spanish vocabulary is shrinking, and when her grandparents visit from Mexico, Sofia struggles to hold a conversation with them.

This shift is devastating for the family. Daniel feels that they are losing an essential part of their identity, and Miriam worries that

Sofia will grow up disconnected from her heritage. Research confirms that this experience is common – Bearse & de Jong (2008) found that when schools reinforce English dominance, children often perceive their home language as inferior, leading to language attrition and cultural alienation.

The emotional toll on Sofia's parents is profound. They express guilt and helplessness, wondering whether enrolling her in an English-dominant program was the right choice. Yet, they feel pressure from the school, which emphasises that "strong English skills are necessary for success."

Sofia's case underscores a critical issue in ELD: Language loss does not only affect the individual child – it fractures entire families. When home languages are devalued, children may develop a sense of shame around their linguistic heritage, leading to strained familial relationships and a loss of intergenerational knowledge.

To mitigate these harms, schools must adopt bilingual-friendly policies, such as allowing home language use in classrooms, encouraging family language engagement, and incorporating cultural learning into the curriculum. Without these shifts, more families will experience the painful reality of linguistic displacement.

## Case study 3: How bilingual programs impact students' identity and academic outcomes differently

To contrast the challenges of English-only programs, consider the case of two students enrolled in different ELD models:

- Diego, a third grader in a dual-language immersion program, where both English and Spanish are used in instruction.
- Emma, a third grader in an English-only pull-out ESL program, where she receives English language instruction separate from her peers.

After two years in their respective programs, the differences in their linguistic confidence, academic achievement, and sense of identity are striking.

Diego's experience in dual-language education:

- Maintains strong Spanish skills while developing English fluency, leading to higher literacy rates in both languages (Martínez-Álvarez & Chiang, 2020).
- Feels valued in his bilingualism, proudly using Spanish at home and English at school.
- Shows higher academic engagement and better self-esteem due to positive reinforcement of multilingualism.

Emma's experience in English-only ESL:

- Loses proficiency in Spanish, as her school discourages its use, resulting in weaker bilingual literacy (Küppers, 2022).
- Experiences linguistic insecurity, feeling "not good enough" in either English or Spanish.
- Struggles with academic content since she cannot fully engage with complex material in either language.

Diego's case illustrates how dual-language programs foster academic and emotional well-being, whereas Emma's case highlights the harm of subtractive bilingualism – where English is gained at the cost of the home language. These findings align with research showing that bilingual students in well-supported programs outperform their monolingual peers across cognitive and linguistic domains (Küppers, 2022).

The key takeaway? ELD models that integrate home languages create stronger academic outcomes and a healthier sense of identity, while English-only approaches increase the risk of language loss, disengagement, and cultural disconnection.

### Reflection questions

After reading these cases, consider the following:

- What can these cases teach us about the role of identity in language learning?
- How might teachers mediate the identity challenges evidenced in the cases?
- What small but meaningful changes could be made in existing ELD programs to better support multilingual learners? (*Think about adjustments you could make within your current role or context, even if broader systemic reform feels out of reach.*)

The next section will explore the benefits of home language integration, presenting research-backed strategies for preserving linguistic diversity in classrooms.

## The benefits of home language integration

The previous section illustrated how language suppression impacts multilingual learners, leading to academic struggles, cultural disconnection, and identity crises. However, research consistently shows that maintaining and integrating home languages in educational spaces benefits students both linguistically and emotionally.

By shifting from language replacement models to language inclusion models, educators can foster stronger academic outcomes, greater cognitive flexibility, and a deeper sense of belonging among multilingual students. This section explores these benefits through two key lenses: linguistic development and cultural pride.

## Linguistic benefits of home language maintenance

Contrary to the belief that bilingualism interferes with English acquisition, research demonstrates that maintaining the home language enhances overall linguistic and cognitive development. Van Laere & Braak (2014) found that students who continue to develop their first language exhibit stronger literacy skills, higher academic achievement, and greater problem-solving abilities compared to those who experience home language loss.

This phenomenon is explained by the interdependence hypothesis, which suggests that proficiency in one language supports the development of another. When students retain and strengthen their home language, they transfer foundational literacy and cognitive skills to English, making academic learning more accessible.

For example:

- Bilingual students often develop greater metalinguistic awareness, meaning they can understand and manipulate language structures more effectively than monolingual peers (Linse, 2013).

- Cognitive flexibility is heightened in students who actively use multiple languages, improving
- Bilingual learners have a long-term academic advantage, particularly in subjects requiring analytical thinking, such as mathematics and science (Daud, 2024).

Moreover, home language integration reduces the cognitive burden placed on students in English-only classrooms. Instead of struggling to process complex academic concepts in a language they have not yet fully mastered, multilingual students benefit from using their strongest language as a foundation for deeper comprehension.

For instance, in dual-language programs, students engage with subjects in both their home language and English, leading to higher retention rates and better overall academic performance (Linse, 2013). This is particularly critical in math, science, and social studies, where conceptual understanding is more important than rote memorisation of English vocabulary.

Simply put: When schools value and incorporate home languages, students learn better, retain more information, and develop stronger academic skills.

## Cultural pride and a sense of belonging

Beyond cognitive and academic benefits, home language integration plays a crucial role in shaping students' cultural identity and self-esteem. When students are encouraged to maintain and use their home language, they develop a greater sense of pride in their heritage, reinforcing their social confidence and emotional well-being (Mak et al., 2023).

Bilingual programs provide safe spaces where multilingual learners feel valued – not just as English learners, but as individuals with rich linguistic and cultural backgrounds. Linse (2013) found that students in classrooms that embrace home languages are more engaged, participate more actively, and show higher levels of motivation.

A compelling example of this can be seen in students enrolled in dual-language immersion programs, where both English and the home language are equally prioritised. These students frequently outperform their monolingual peers academically while also exhibiting higher self-esteem and stronger social connections (Daud, 2024).

Consider the story of Amara, a fifth-grade student in a Spanish-English dual-language program. Initially, she struggled with identity conflicts – at home, she spoke Spanish fluently, but at school, she felt pressure to use only English. However, after being placed in a program that affirmed her bilingualism, Amara's academic confidence flourished. She began participating more in class, forming stronger peer relationships, and proudly embracing her identity as a bilingual learner.

This experience is not unique. Culturally responsive education that integrates home languages validates students' lived experiences, fostering:

- Greater confidence in their abilities as learners
- Stronger social bonds with peers and family members
- A positive self-concept as multilingual individuals

Conversely, students in English-only classrooms often experience the opposite effect – a decline in self-esteem, reduced participation, and a gradual detachment from their cultural identity (Mak et al., 2023).

## Summary

The benefits of home language integration in schools are undeniable. Bilingual students gain stronger academic skills, greater cognitive flexibility, and a reinforced sense of cultural belonging. Schools that prioritise dual-language learning and home language support create environments where multilingual students can thrive, rather than struggle against a system designed for monolinguals.

The next section will focus on practical strategies for supporting home languages in classrooms and communities, exploring how teachers, families, and policymakers can work together to ensure linguistic equity in education.

# Practical strategies for supporting home languages

The previous section highlighted the academic, cognitive, and emotional benefits of maintaining home languages in schools. However, simply acknowledging these benefits is not enough – educators, families, and policymakers must take concrete action to ensure that multilingual students receive the support they need.

This section presents three key strategies for fostering home language development: classroom practices, community engagement, and policy advocacy. By implementing these approaches, schools can shift from linguistic suppression to linguistic empowerment, creating an environment where multilingualism is embraced as a strength rather than treated as an obstacle.

## Classroom practices: Creating space for home languages in learning

Teachers play a critical role in shaping students' language identities, and even small adjustments to classroom practice – when made intentionally – can make a meaningful difference in validating and integrating home languages. Acharya (2022) argues that when educators actively incorporate students' home languages into instruction, it not only enhances academic learning but also fosters a sense of belonging and cultural pride. While some of these shifts may appear simple on the surface, they often require a deeper transformation in ideology, mindset, and pedagogical approach – particularly for teachers whose training or experience has centred monolingual norms. Acknowledging this complexity can create space for more honest reflection and sustained growth.

Some effective strategies include:

- Encouraging students to use their home language in learning activities:
  - o Translanguaging techniques: Allowing students to take notes, brainstorm ideas, or discuss concepts in their home language before transitioning to English.
  - o Multilingual writing assignments: Inviting students to draft stories, reflections, or research in both English and their home language.
- Integrating cultural narratives into instruction:

- o Bilingual storytelling and literature: Using books and folktales from students' cultural backgrounds to reinforce literacy skills in both languages (Gray, 1998).
- o Oral history projects: Assigning students to interview family members in their home language, then presenting findings in both English and their native tongue.

- Valuing linguistic diversity in classroom discussions:
    - o Multilingual word walls: Displaying key vocabulary in multiple languages to affirm all linguistic backgrounds.
    - o Language-sharing moments: Encouraging students to teach their classmates words and phrases in their home languages, fostering peer learning.

These practices normalise bilingualism and multilingualism in the classroom, showing students that their home language is not something to hide but rather a valuable academic and cultural resource.

## Community engagement: Strengthening home language use beyond the classroom

While classroom strategies are vital, true home language integration extends beyond school walls. Families play a crucial role in reinforcing bilingual development, but many immigrant and multilingual parents feel disconnected from the school system due to language barriers or past experiences of marginalisation (Zhang & Jiang, 2024). At the same time, some upwardly mobile or acculturated families may actively discourage the use of a home language, viewing exclusive English use as a pathway to academic and economic success. These decisions are often shaped by internalised societal pressures, fear of stigmatisation, or a desire to protect children from discrimination. Schools must recognise these varied realities and proactively partner with families and communities in ways that affirm linguistic diversity without imposing a one-size-fits-all approach – creating a support system that honours multiple entry points into bilingual identity and practice.

Some effective approaches include:

- Inviting families into home-language-centred activities in flexible ways:
  - Hosting bilingual family literacy nights, where parents and children can read, write, and discuss books in their home language together if they choose.
  - Providing multilingual newsletters and resources, ensuring that families receive school communications in their preferred language.
- Creating opportunities for community-based language immersion:
  - Inviting elders and community leaders to share traditional stories, songs, or lessons in students' home languages – offering students cultural connection points even if families are navigating complex relationships to their linguistic heritage.
  - Forming multilingual student mentorship programs, where older bilingual students support younger learners in both academic and social settings.
- Supporting families in maintaining or reconnecting with bilingualism where desired:
  - Schools can offer guidance to parents on the benefits of maintaining bilingualism at home, while recognising

that attitudes towards home language use vary and may be shaped by experiences of marginalisation or assimilation pressure.

- o Providing optional multilingual homework assignments that involve family participation – such as interviewing a relative in their home language and then translating key points into English – can allow for meaningful engagement without mandating it.

When schools engage families and communities in linguistically inclusive ways – grounded in respect for differing values and histories – students are more likely to experience a reinforced sense of pride in their multilingual identity. These collaborative practices help make language maintenance not only possible but sustainable.

## Policy advocacy: Institutional changes for multilingual equity

While teachers and families can take immediate action, systemic change requires policy advocacy to ensure that home languages are protected at an institutional level. Soltero-González (2009) emphasises that without structural support – such as dual-language programs, bilingual teacher training, and multilingual learning resources – individual classroom efforts may have limited long-term impact.

Key areas for advocacy include:

- Expanding dual-language education programs:
  - o Schools should prioritise bilingual and dual-language immersion models rather than defaulting to English-only instruction.

  - Policymakers must allocate funding for bilingual education, ensuring that students have access to qualified teachers, bilingual curricula, and appropriate learning materials.
- Challenging English-only mandates:
  - Many schools still operate under restrictive language policies that discourage home language use. Advocating for multilingual-friendly policies can help dismantle these outdated restrictions.
  - Schools should offer formal home language support, such as bilingual assessments and instructional accommodations for students who are still developing English proficiency.
- Training educators in multilingual and culturally responsive teaching:
  - Many teachers receive limited training in bilingual education, leaving them unsure of how to support multilingual learners effectively.
  - Advocacy efforts should push for teacher professional development programs that focus on translanguaging strategies, linguistic equity, and multilingual student engagement (Zhang & Jiang, 2024).

By addressing policy-level barriers, schools can ensure that language integration is not dependent on individual educators' willingness to accommodate students, but rather a fundamental principle of the education system.

## Summary

The strategies outlined above offer practical steps for integrating home languages into schools, communities, and policy frameworks. By implementing these approaches, educators and policymakers can reverse the harm caused by English-only models and create learning environments where multilingual students thrive.

However, effective language education requires more than just policy shifts – it also demands critical self-reflection from educators. The next section will invite teachers to assess their own linguistic biases, consider how their classroom practices shape students' language identities, and explore ways to become more inclusive educators.

## Reflection and self-assessment for educators

The previous sections have demonstrated how language policies, instructional practices, and community engagement shape multilingual students' academic and personal experiences. However, institutional change begins with self-reflection at the individual level. Educators must critically examine their assumptions about language, identity, and learning to ensure that their classrooms support rather than suppress linguistic diversity.

### Critical reflection: Examining language bias in teaching

Many teachers, often unconsciously, operate under the assumption that English proficiency is the ultimate measure of academic success. This belief is deeply embedded in TESOL-based ELD models, where home languages are treated as temporary stepping stones rather than valuable lifelong assets (Daly & Sharma, 2018).

To begin reflecting on your own approach, consider the following questions:

1. How do your language expectations shape student participation?
    a. How does your current approach to classroom language use affect students' comfort and confidence in drawing on their home languages?
    b. How do you react when students speak in a language other than English?
2. How do you integrate cultural and linguistic diversity into instruction?
    a. Do your lesson plans include materials that reflect multilingual perspectives?
    b. Do you encourage students to share and celebrate their linguistic backgrounds?
3. How do you support multilingual students beyond language instruction?
    a. Do you provide resources that affirm students' home languages?
    b. How do you engage with families to ensure they feel included in their child's learning?

Honest reflection is the first step towards making meaningful changes in the classroom. By shifting from an assimilationist mindset to an inclusion-based approach, educators can ensure that students feel valued for who they are, rather than pressured to conform to monolingual norms (Cheatham, Jiménez-Silva, & Park, 2015).

## Classroom activity: Designing a culturally inclusive lesson

To actively integrate home languages into instruction, consider designing a lesson that affirms multilingual identity.

Lesson objective:

To explore students' linguistic and cultural identities through storytelling.

Activity: "My language, my story"

1. Students write or record a short story or memory in their home language (if they are comfortable doing so).
2. They translate or explain their story in English, focusing on meaning rather than direct word-for-word translation.
3. Classmates engage in discussions, asking questions about the cultural significance of the stories and sharing their own experiences.
4. Students reflect on what they learned about each other's languages and traditions.

Why this works:

- Encourages multilingual expression while reinforcing literacy skills.
- Fosters peer learning by allowing students to engage with multiple languages.
- Strengthens cultural pride by creating space for home languages in an academic setting.

Educators can adapt this activity across subjects and grade levels, using bilingual projects, multilingual peer collaborations, and oral storytelling traditions to create a more inclusive learning environment.

### Summary

Through self-reflection and intentional instructional design, teachers can shift from language gatekeepers to language allies. Recognising the value of multilingualism and actively creating linguistically affirming classrooms ensures that students can thrive academically without losing their cultural and linguistic roots.

The next and final section will synthesise the key insights from this chapter, reinforcing the importance of moving from monolingual assumptions to multilingual empowerment in education.

## Bridge to chapter 3

Throughout this chapter, we have examined the crucial role of home language in identity formation, the damaging effects of language suppression, and the benefits of integrating multilingualism into education. We have also explored practical strategies for fostering home language development, ensuring that multilingual learners are not forced to choose between academic success and cultural belonging.

However, language acquisition is not a one-size-fits-all process. While many students struggle with the pressures of English-only instruction, some face additional challenges due to differences in neurological processing. In particular, GLPs – individuals who acquire and use language in holistic chunks rather than through traditional grammatical structures – require unique educational approaches to support their language learning.

Chapter 3 will explore how Gestalt Language Processors navigate ELD programs, examining both the challenges they face and the opportunities for tailored support. Many current ELD models rely on analytical language processing assumptions, which can unintentionally hinder GLPs' ability to develop both English and their home language effectively. By understanding the diversity of language processing styles, educators can create more inclusive learning environments that accommodate both neurodivergence and multilingualism.

In the next chapter, we will:

- Define Gestalt Language Processing and its implications for multilingual learners.
- Explore how current ELD practices fail to support GLPs.
- Identify effective strategies for fostering language development in neurodivergent students.

By expanding our understanding of how different minds acquire and use language, we can move closer to a truly inclusive and equitable approach to language education.

## Summary and application across age groups

The integration of home languages into educational spaces must be responsive not only to cultural and linguistic diversity but also to the developmental stages of learners. In early childhood settings, language-rich environments that include bilingual storytelling, songs, and play-based translanguaging lay the foundation for strong linguistic identity. Primary school students benefit from structured opportunities to use their home language alongside English in literacy and content areas, reinforcing academic concepts while affirming cultural pride. At the secondary level, students can engage in more complex multilingual projects – such as oral histories, comparative literature analysis, and bilingual research presentations – that deepen both academic understanding and cultural connection. By tailoring strategies to students' developmental needs, educators can ensure that home language integration is meaningful and accessible across grade levels.

## Key takeaways

- Home language is integral to identity formation, fostering cultural pride, familial bonds, and psychological well-being.
- English-only ELD models often erode home language use, leading to identity crises, academic struggles, and cultural disconnection.
- Dual-language and bilingual programs support stronger academic outcomes, cognitive flexibility, and higher student engagement than English-only models.
- Practical strategies – such as translanguaging, multilingual materials, and family engagement – can be adapted across age groups to support home language maintenance.
- Educators, families, and policymakers must collaborate to shift from assimilationist approaches to inclusive, multilingual educational frameworks.

By applying these insights thoughtfully, educators can create classrooms where multilingual students are empowered to thrive both academically and culturally.

# 3 Gestalt Language Processors in the ELD classroom

## Learning objectives

- Understand Gestalt Language Processors (GLPs) and their unique language acquisition processes.
- Recognise the challenges GLPs face in traditional ELD frameworks designed for Analytical Language Processors.
- Explore strategies to support GLPs within the context of decolonised, inclusive ELD practices.

## Rationale

The learning goals of this chapter are grounded in the urgent need to recognise and accommodate the diverse language acquisition processes of GLPs within ELD classrooms. Traditional ELD frameworks, rooted in assumptions of analytical language processing, fail to meet the needs of GLPs whose natural linguistic development relies on holistic, context-rich, and pattern-based learning. These goals aim to illuminate the challenges GLPs face when subjected to rigid, monolingual, and grammar-focused instruction, particularly within TESOL models designed for ALPs. By understanding the unique trajectory of GLPs and the compounded barriers they encounter as multilingual and often neurodiverse learners, educators can begin to shift towards a decolonised, inclusive pedagogy. This chapter offers not only a critique of existing frameworks but also practical, context-driven strategies for supporting GLPs – emphasising the necessity of translanguaging, home language integration, and culturally responsive teaching. The objectives thus serve as a guide for reimagining ELD as a liberatory space where all learners, regardless of neurotype or linguistic background, are empowered to thrive.

## Introduction: Who are Gestalt Language Processors?

Language development varies significantly across individuals, and one of the most overlooked distinctions in educational settings is between Gestalt Language Processors and Analytical Language Processors. Traditional ELD frameworks are designed with the assumption that all learners acquire language analytically – building meaning from individual words and phrases. However, GLPs follow a different developmental trajectory, one that prioritises whole phrases, intonation patterns, and scripts before breaking language into smaller, flexible units.

This distinction has profound implications for multilingual learners and neurodiverse students in ELD classrooms. While GLPs represent a significant portion of the language-learning population, they are often mischaracterised as struggling or delayed because their language acquisition does not align with standard educational models. Recognising their unique processing style is essential for fostering an inclusive, equitable approach to ELD instruction.

## Defining GLPs and their language acquisition process

GLPs acquire language in chunks rather than through individual word learning. Instead of constructing sentences piece by piece, they process and store entire phrases – a phenomenon known as echolalia, which is the first stage of the Natural Language Acquisition (NLA) framework (Blanc, Blackwell, & Elias, 2023). Over time, they modify these scripts, gradually breaking them down into flexible components that can be recombined into novel utterances.

Key stages of GLP language acquisition include:

- Echolalia (Stage 1) – Immediate or delayed repetition of entire phrases heard from others.
- Mitigated Gestalts (Stage 2–3) – Slight modifications to stored scripts, adapting phrases for different contexts.
- Single-word separation (Stage 4) – Extracting individual words from memorised phrases.
- Self-generated language (Stage 5–6) – Independently constructing novel sentences and flexible language use.

Unlike ALPs, who develop syntax and grammar early on, GLPs may appear to have "advanced" language skills at first due to their ability to recall and use complex phrases, but their comprehension and ability to generate original speech often lag behind. This can lead to misunderstandings in assessment and intervention, particularly in ELD contexts where structured language instruction is designed for ALPs (Blanc et al., 2023).

## GLPs in ELD contexts: Overlooked and misunderstood

The dominant TESOL/ELD frameworks are largely designed for ALPs, assuming that students will acquire English by learning isolated vocabulary, grammar rules, and phonetic structures before forming sentences. This linear, word-based approach does not align with how GLPs acquire language, often making ELD instruction feel inaccessible or ineffective for these learners.

Why traditional ELD fails GLPs:

- Rigid curriculum sequencing – Teaching individual words and grammar first does not align with GLP acquisition patterns.
- Assessment bias – Standard tests measure isolated language skills, failing to capture gestalt learning.
- Lack of multi-sensory or contextual support – GLPs learn best in environments where language is tied to meaningful, immersive contexts, such as storytelling or interactive role-playing (Keiko, 2008).

Additionally, many GLPs are neurodiverse and multilingual, meaning they are already managing multiple language systems in a way that defies conventional teaching expectations. In ELD settings, these learners are often seen as struggling when, in reality, they require different instructional strategies that honour their natural processing style (Mezzadri, 2022). Without recognition of their learning needs, they are at risk of being misdiagnosed with language impairments or being pushed towards interventions that prioritise rote learning rather than authentic language engagement.

## The need for a paradigm shift

The failure to accommodate GLPs in ELD classrooms perpetuates inequities in language education. A one-size-fits-all approach does not work for diverse learners, and understanding GLP acquisition patterns is essential for developing inclusive, effective instructional strategies. By reframing ELD through a lens that acknowledges Gestalt processing, educators can create environments where all multilingual learners – whether they process language in typical or non-typical ways – are given the tools they need to thrive.

This chapter lays the groundwork for a deeper exploration of how GLPs face systemic barriers in ELD and what can be done to support them more effectively in multilingual, neurodiverse classrooms.

# Challenges GLPs face in ELD classrooms

GLPs encounter significant challenges in traditional ELD classrooms, largely because these programs are designed with ALPs in mind. TESOL and ELD frameworks emphasise a linear, word-by-word approach to language learning, which fails to align with the way GLPs acquire and process language. Additionally, the intersection of neurodiversity and multilingualism compounds these difficulties, as many GLPs are also multilingual learners navigating multiple linguistic systems within environments that prioritise English over home languages. This section explores how these mismatches create barriers to meaningful language development for GLPs.

## Mismatch between GLPs and ELD frameworks

Traditional TESOL and ELD models prioritise isolated vocabulary acquisition, phonetics, and grammar instruction, assuming that learners develop language analytically, piece by piece. However, GLPs process language holistically, storing and retrieving whole phrases or scripts before breaking them into smaller, flexible units (Blanc et al., 2023). This fundamental difference in language acquisition creates a disconnect between instructional practices and how GLPs naturally learn.

Challenges in current ELD frameworks include:

- Word-by-word instruction – Many ELD programs focus on isolated vocabulary instruction – teaching individual words before moving on to full phrases or sentences. This approach assumes that students build language by assembling discrete parts in sequence. However, GLPs acquire language in a top-down fashion, drawing meaning from whole phrases or "chunks" of language first. When instruction is reduced to word lists or flashcards, it deprives GLPs of the contextual and emotional cues they rely on to understand and use language meaningfully.
- Lack of support for echolalia – Echolalia – the repetition of words or phrases previously heard – is often dismissed in ELD classrooms as non-functional or off-task behaviour. For GLPs, however, echolalia is a foundational part of language development. These repeated scripts are not random but serve as building blocks from which spontaneous language later emerges. Without recognising the communicative intent behind echolalia, educators may overlook meaningful

attempts at engagement or prematurely push GLPs towards analytic speech patterns that do not align with how they process language.

- Rigid sequencing of skills – Traditional ELD curricula typically follow a fixed progression: phonics first, then grammar, then sentence structure and composition. This sequence is rooted in Analytic Language Processing (ALP), where learners break language down into component parts. GLPs, by contrast, thrive on immersion in rich, emotionally resonant language contexts. They learn best when they are exposed to full interactions, stories, or songs – where meaning is conveyed holistically – before breaking down the details of structure. Rigid sequencing prevents them from accessing language in ways that align with their strengths and needs (Papapostolou, Manoli, & Mouti, 2020).

Because GLPs do not follow the linear trajectory prescribed by conventional ELD frameworks, they are often misidentified as struggling or behind. In reality, they require different instructional strategies that build on their strengths – such as a sensitivity to patterns, rhythm, and emotional tone. When interventions are based exclusively on ALP models, GLPs may experience ongoing frustration, disengagement, and a sense that language learning is beyond their reach – not because they lack ability, but because the system fails to meet them where they are.

## Intersection of neurodiversity and multilingualism

The challenges GLPs face in ELD classrooms are further compounded when they are also multilingual learners. Many GLPs process multiple languages in ways that defy traditional assumptions about second-language acquisition. Rather than learning one language analytically before acquiring another, GLPs tend to absorb linguistic patterns across multiple languages simultaneously, often mixing elements of their home language(s) and English in ways that can appear disjointed within conventional assessment frameworks (Machaba, Sipholi, & Motseki, 2024).

Key barriers multilingual GLPs face in ELD classrooms include:

- Lack of translanguaging instructional approaches – Many ELD programs discourage mixing languages, even though GLPs benefit from drawing on their full linguistic repertoire when developing English proficiency.
- Rigid assessment standards – Standardised language assessments prioritise isolated word recall and grammar knowledge, which disadvantages GLPs who rely on context-driven language use (Solis & Flores-Chang, 2024).
- Overemphasis on written language – GLPs often excel in spoken, patterned language but struggle with rigid written structures, particularly when home-language literacy development is not supported alongside English instruction.

Instead of embracing GLPs' natural tendency to engage with multiple languages holistically, ELD frameworks often position non-standard language use – such as echolalia, code-switching, or non-linear sentence construction – as signs of deficiency. This deficit-oriented lens creates multiple barriers for multilingual, neurodiverse learners. For example, students may be excluded from advanced language tracks due to perceived "delays" in grammatical mastery, or their scripted language may be misinterpreted as a behavioural issue rather than a legitimate form of communication. Standardised assessments rooted in analytic language models may fail to capture their comprehension and expressive capacity, leading to inaccurate placement or the denial of services. These practices reinforce systemic inequities in language education, particularly for students whose natural linguistic patterns do not conform to traditional ALP expectations, and who are often left without the supports needed to thrive.

## Recognising the need for a shift in ELD practices

GLPs, particularly those who are multilingual, require a fundamental shift in ELD instructional design. Current models fail to account for the diversity of language processing styles, leaving GLPs at a disadvantage. Without an approach that acknowledges the value of echolalia, pattern-based learning, and translanguaging, GLPs are mischaracterised as struggling rather than recognised for their unique strengths. The following sections will explore how context-based, multilingual approaches can better support GLPs within ELD classrooms.

## The power of context: Supporting GLPs through TEFL-inspired practices

GLPs thrive in environments where language is meaningful, contextual, and tied to real-life experiences. Unlike ALPs, who can build language from individual words and grammar rules, GLPs rely on situational and patterned language exposure to develop fluency. This makes rote memorisation and isolated vocabulary drills ineffective, as these methods strip language of the contextual cues GLPs need to understand and use it effectively (Keiko, 2008).

Traditional ELD programs, grounded in TESOL methodologies, often focus on explicit grammar instruction and sequential language learning, which can alienate GLPs. A TEFL-inspired approach, which views English as a situational tool rather than a rigid system, offers a more effective way to support GLPs in ELD settings. By embedding language learning in interactive, immersive, and socially meaningful contexts, educators can create environments that align with how GLPs naturally acquire and process language.

## Why context matters for GLPs

Language learning for GLPs is most successful when it occurs in meaningful, interactive situations. Situational English instruction – where language is learned within the context of real-world interactions – better supports GLPs' gestalt processing than rigid, rule-based methods (Anuyahong & Songakul, 2024).

Key advantages of context-based learning for GLPs include:

- Enhanced comprehension – GLPs extract meaning from patterns, tone, and rhythm, making contextual exposure more effective than explicit grammar instruction.
- Improved retention – Real-world interactions provide emotionally significant moments, reinforcing language in ways that rote memorisation does not.
- Greater engagement – Interactive methods such as storytelling, conversation-based learning, and role-playing tap into GLPs' natural strengths.

By shifting away from static worksheets and isolated vocabulary drills, educators can provide situational learning experiences that allow GLPs to engage with language in a way that feels natural and accessible (Simarmata, 2024).

## Practical applications for contextual learning

To effectively teach GLPs, educators must incorporate interactive, multimodal approaches that align with how these learners process language. Many of these TEFL-inspired strategies – such as using story, rhythm, movement, and visual scaffolds – not only support GLPs, but also reflect sound pedagogical principles that benefit a wide range of learners. In fact, such practices are foundational in alternative models like Waldorf education and can help reclaim expressive, relational, and creative modes of learning that have often been sidelined in mainstream classrooms.

- Storytelling and narratives
  - Encouraging students to engage with language through meaningful, repetitive story structures.
  - Using familiar, scripted interactions to build comprehension and flexible language use.
- Role-playing and real-world scenarios
  - Practicing structured social interactions, such as ordering food, asking for directions, or participating in interviews.
  - Embedding vocabulary within relevant, culturally meaningful exchanges rather than isolated word drills.
- Translanguaging as a scaffold
  - Allowing students to mix home language(s) with English in a way that supports holistic meaning-making.

- o Recognising that GLPs often process multiple languages at once and should not be forced into monolingual structures (Wang, 2018).

By integrating these dynamic, TEFL-inspired approaches, educators can bridge the gap between how GLPs naturally acquire language and how they are traditionally taught in ELD settings. Recognising the power of context in language learning is key to creating equitable, effective instruction for multilingual and neurodiverse learners.

## Integrating home languages into GLP support

GLPs benefit immensely from multi-language input, yet most ELD programs fail to acknowledge the critical role of home language in their development. Traditional English-only approaches assume that exposure to multiple languages confuses learners, but research suggests bilingual and multilingual support enhances both BICS and CALP (Pacheco, David, & Jiménez, 2015). For GLPs, home language provides a critical scaffold for making sense of English, supporting natural language acquisition rather than disrupting it.

Despite this, home languages are often discouraged in ELD classrooms, with students expected to learn English in isolation from their native linguistic environment. This practice contradicts research showing that language processing – especially in GLPs – thrives when multiple linguistic systems are reinforced simultaneously (Mitits, Alexiou, & Milton, 2018). Instead of viewing home languages as barriers to English acquisition, educators should recognise them as essential tools for supporting language development.

## The role of home language in GLPs' development

GLPs naturally process language in patterns, intonation, and rhythm, meaning their ability to transfer skills between languages is stronger than conventional ELD approaches acknowledge. When GLPs have access to their home language, they are better able to decode and construct meaning in English. Research highlights several benefits of bilingual language development for GLPs:

- Enhanced CALP development – Strong home-language skills accelerate the ability to engage with academic English, rather than delaying it (Caddy, 2015).
- Improved comprehension and retention – Multilingual exposure reinforces patterns in English by allowing GLPs to map familiar linguistic structures onto new ones.
- More authentic engagement – Allowing students to use their full linguistic repertoire fosters a sense of identity, agency, and cultural pride.

Rather than focusing solely on English, an inclusive ELD model should integrate home language as a bridge to English proficiency, ensuring that students' linguistic and cultural backgrounds remain assets rather than obstacles.

## Practical classroom strategies

To support GLPs effectively, educators must create home-language-inclusive classrooms that align with their natural learning processes. Key strategies include:

- Using home language–based echolalia
    - Many GLPs store and retrieve language in chunks, meaning they naturally borrow from their home language while acquiring English.
    - Teachers can leverage this by encouraging students to make connections between memorised phrases in both languages, rather than forcing them into a monolingual structure.
- Encouraging cultural and linguistic pride
    - Affirming students' home languages in the classroom enhances engagement and validates their linguistic identities (Zhang & Jiang, 2024).
    - Allowing multilingual storytelling, translanguaging activities, and bilingual text discussions ensures that GLPs' full linguistic abilities are acknowledged and nurtured.

By integrating home language as a core component of ELD instruction, educators can align teaching with GLPs' natural language processing strengths, rather than forcing them into models designed for ALPs. Supporting GLPs through home language integration also fosters development across both BICS and CALP. Access to familiar linguistic structures enables GLPs to engage more confidently in social communication (BICS), while reinforcing patterns and meanings that transfer to academic contexts (CALP). Rather than hindering English acquisition, bilingual support accelerates deeper, more meaningful language development. Recognising the value of bilingualism in gestalt processing is key to creating inclusive and effective ELD environments.

# Culturally responsive practices for GLPs in ELD

Historically, ELD has been framed through an assimilationist lens, where success is measured by how quickly students conform to monolingual, standardised language norms. This deficit-based perspective disproportionately harms GLPs, who naturally acquire language through holistic, patterned, and contextual learning rather than analytical, rule-driven instruction. A culturally responsive approach to ELD must recognise and value GLPs' diverse linguistic and cognitive strengths, rather than forcing them into models designed for ALPs (Orosco & Abdulrahim, 2017).

By decolonising ELD, educators can move away from rigid, prescriptive teaching methods that fail GLPs and instead adopt strength-based, flexible approaches that honour students' cultural and linguistic identities.

## Decolonising ELD for GLPs

A decolonised approach to ELD shifts away from monolingual, standardised expectations and embraces linguistic diversity as an asset, not a barrier. GLPs, particularly those from multilingual or indigenous backgrounds, have historically been marginalised in education systems that prioritise rigid English-only instruction (Garza, Lavigne, & Si, 2020). A culturally responsive model reframes these students as integral to a diverse classroom ecosystem, rather than positioning them as struggling or behind.

Key shifts in mindset include:

- Recognising linguistic diversity as an advantage – Rather than penalising students for non-standard English use, educators should embrace translanguaging and multi-language scaffolding.

- Honouring alternative language processing styles – A GLP-friendly ELD framework should prioritise meaningful, story-driven, and pattern-based instruction over grammar drills.
- Centering student agency – Allowing students to express themselves in ways that feel natural rather than forcing rigid linguistic structures.

This strength-based approach aligns with neurodiverse students' learning needs, ensuring that GLPs are not seen as deficits to be fixed, but as learners with unique and valuable linguistic assets (Santamaría, 2009).

## Culturally responsive examples

Successful culturally responsive classrooms adapt teaching to align with students' lived experiences, linguistic strengths, and cultural identities. Several case studies illustrate how this works in practice:

### Dual-language, GLP-inclusive classrooms

A bilingual school in New Mexico integrated storytelling and music-based language acquisition for Spanish-speaking GLPs, allowing them to develop both Spanish and English through pattern-rich, narrative-driven instruction (Torres-Velásquez & Lobo, 2004).

Instead of penalising echolalic speech, teachers built on students' natural repetition patterns, helping them transition from memorised scripts to flexible communication.

### Indigenous and community-centered language learning

In classrooms serving Indigenous students, teachers used culturally relevant stories and oral traditions to teach English, rather than enforcing rote memorisation of grammar rules (Garza, Lavigne, & Si, 2020).

Students were encouraged to blend home languages with English, reinforcing the idea that all linguistic knowledge is valuable.

By adopting culturally responsive, GLP-affirming ELD strategies, educators can create more inclusive, equitable learning environments that recognise and honour linguistic diversity. Rather than forcing GLPs to fit outdated models of language instruction, decolonised ELD frameworks provide the flexibility and respect necessary for all learners to thrive.

## Tools and techniques for supporting GLPs

Supporting GLPs in ELD classrooms requires tools and assessment methods that align with their natural language development processes. Many traditional instructional resources and evaluation frameworks are designed for ALPs, assuming linear, rule-based language acquisition. However, GLPs thrive when provided with multimodal, interactive learning tools and assessment methods that capture their holistic approach to language processing.

Here, we explore technological resources for educators and alternative assessment strategies that better reflect GLPs' linguistic strengths.

### Resources for teachers: Tools to support GLPs

Assistive technologies and multimodal supports are essential for creating an inclusive, responsive ELD environment. Visual, auditory, and interactive tools provide the necessary context for GLPs to process and store language meaningfully.

Key tools include:

- Visual aids and graphic organisers – Charts, mind maps, and illustrated story sequences help GLPs connect language to patterns and imagery, reinforcing comprehension (Monsores, Almeida, Quadros, & Quadros, 2020).
- Interactive language applications – Programs that allow learners to hear and mimic phrases (e.g., AI-driven conversation apps) align with gestalt processing by reinforcing phrase-based learning (Percovich, Tosi, Chiruzzo, & Rosá, 2019).
- Gesture- and movement-based learning – Embodied learning, such as acting out phrases or using sign language alongside speech, enhances retention by pairing language with physical action.

In addition to technological tools, professional development for teachers is crucial. Training modules should focus on:

- Identifying GLPs in the classroom – Helping educators recognise echolalia, chunk-based learning, and holistic processing patterns.
- Differentiated instructional strategies – Providing concrete methods for scaffolding ELD instruction for GLPs, rather than applying standard ALP-based approaches (Puustinen, Baker, & Lund, 2006).

## Assessment redesign: Measuring GLPs' progress holistically

Traditional standardised assessments focus on isolated vocabulary recall, grammar rules, and written responses, which often misrepresent GLPs' actual language abilities. Instead of forcing GLPs into ALP-based evaluation methods, assessment should reflect how they naturally develop and use language.

Key alternative assessment strategies include:

- Performance-based assessments – Instead of fill-in-the-blank tests, GLPs demonstrate comprehension through role-playing, storytelling, or real-world language use.
- Portfolio-based tracking – Collecting audio recordings, video samples, and written work over time provides a more accurate picture of GLPs' evolving language skills.
- Flexible response options – Allowing oral responses, visual representations, or multimodal explanations ensures assessments accommodate GLPs' strengths in contextual communication.

By shifting away from rigid testing towards dynamic, student-centered evaluation, educators can accurately measure GLPs' language growth while validating their unique learning styles. These tools and assessment methods not only empower GLPs but also contribute to a more inclusive, equitable ELD framework.

## Bridging theory and practice

Understanding GLPs in ELD classrooms requires more than just awareness – it demands a shift in instructional approaches, assessment models, and educator mindsets. The previous chapters have outlined the challenges GLPs face in traditional ELD settings, the importance of contextual learning and home language integration, and culturally responsive practices that affirm linguistic diversity. However, to truly support GLPs, educators must actively reflect on their teaching practices and challenge the assumptions that reinforce deficit-based models.

### Reflective prompts for educators

To begin this process, educators can consider the following questions:

- How do my current teaching practices accommodate GLPs?
  - Do I provide situational, meaningful language exposure rather than isolated vocabulary drills?
  - Am I incorporating multimodal, interactive strategies that align with gestalt processing?
- What assumptions about language processing might I need to challenge?
  - Do I expect all students to learn English through an analytical, word-by-word approach?
  - Am I unintentionally prioritising monolingualism over multilingual strengths?

Reflecting on these questions allows educators to identify areas for growth and adjust their instructional methods to create a more inclusive and effective ELD environment.

## Looking ahead

Chapter 4 will expand on the concept of decolonising ELD, moving beyond GLP-specific concerns to examine how the entire field of English language education must shift towards equity and liberation. It will explore:

- The historical roots of assimilationist language policies in ELD
- The harm of English-centric instruction and monolingual bias

- A reimagined, student-centered approach that values linguistic diversity

By bridging theory and practice, educators can work towards an ELD framework that is not only accessible for GLPs but also liberatory for all multilingual learners.

# Summary

This chapter explored the unique language acquisition processes of GLPs and the systemic challenges they face within traditional ELD frameworks designed for ALPs. By examining the mismatch between rigid, monolingual instructional models and the holistic, pattern-based learning style of GLPs, this chapter underscored the need for a paradigm shift in language education. TEFL-inspired, context-driven practices, translanguaging, and home language integration emerged as key strategies to support GLPs in multilingual, neurodiverse classrooms. Culturally responsive, decolonised pedagogy was presented as essential for recognising the strengths of GLPs and ensuring that all learners – regardless of neurotype or linguistic background – can thrive in ELD settings.

## Key takeaways

- GLPs acquire language holistically through scripts, patterns, and context, not through isolated word learning and grammar instruction.
- Traditional TESOL/ELD frameworks are misaligned with GLP needs, often mischaracterising their learning as delayed or deficient.
- Contextual, interactive learning environments support GLPs' natural language development, while rote and linear instruction hinders it.

- Translanguaging and home language integration are vital for GLPs, enhancing comprehension, identity affirmation, and academic engagement.
- Culturally responsive, decolonised ELD practices recognise linguistic diversity as an asset, affirming GLPs' processing styles and cultural backgrounds.
- Alternative assessments and multimodal tools more accurately reflect GLPs' language skills, supporting equitable evaluation of progress.

Supporting GLPs in ELD classrooms requires more than accommodation – it demands a fundamental reimagining of language education that honours diverse ways of learning. By embracing inclusive, context-rich, and culturally affirming practices, educators can transform ELD from a site of marginalisation into one of empowerment for all multilingual, neurodiverse learners.

# 4

# Decolonising ELD: Uplifting CALP in home and target languages

## Learning objectives

- Recognise the differences in CALP growth between Gestalt and Analytic Language Processors.
- Learn strategies for holistic language instruction that address both processing types and accommodate multiple home languages or dialects.
- Develop methods for teaching CALP in home languages even when the teacher lacks academic fluency in those languages.
- Understand the global benefits of home language CALP for higher education and career opportunities.

## Rationale

This chapter addresses the critical need to support the development of CALP in both home and target languages, particularly for learners with diverse language processing styles. Too often, ELD instruction centers English at the expense of students' home languages, undermining academic growth and reinforcing systemic inequities. Furthermore, instructional practices typically assume analytic language processing, leaving GLPs without meaningful access to academic language. By recognising the global importance of home language CALP, this chapter aims to equip educators with strategies for holistic, inclusive instruction that honours linguistic diversity and neurodiversity. Whether teachers are fluent in students' home languages or not, they can facilitate CALP development through collaborative, context-rich methods that position all learners for academic and professional success in a multilingual world.

## Introduction: Beyond English – the global importance of home language CALP

In language education, the distinction between BICS and CALP is crucial – yet too often, misunderstood or overlooked. Many ELD programs celebrate rapid growth in English BICS, mistaking it for true language proficiency. This premature celebration neglects the slow, deliberate development of CALP, especially when it must be built without a solid foundation in the learner's home language. While BICS may emerge within one to two years, CALP requires sustained support – typically five to seven years – to fully develop. For multilingual learners, home language CALP is not optional; it is essential scaffolding. Without it, English CALP development is fragile, lacking the depth and transferability needed for long-term academic success (Pila & Mavuru, 2022). Additionally, how students develop BICS and CALP varies depending on their language processing style. GLPs tend to acquire BICS and CALP through contextualised, holistic experiences, while ALPs often engage with these proficiencies through structured, rule-based instruction. Recognising these distinct pathways is critical for designing effective, inclusive ELD practices.

The marginalisation of home language instruction undercuts this process, creating learners who are conversationally fluent yet academically adrift. As Mataka, Bhila, and Mukurunge (2020) note, when language in education policy ignores the cognitive development that comes from learning in one's strongest language, learners face significant barriers to academic achievement across subjects. This is particularly harmful in STEM fields, where abstract reasoning and discipline-specific vocabulary require strong CALP foundations. Denying students the opportunity to develop academic proficiency in their home languages limits not only their potential in English-medium education but also their broader cognitive development.

From a global perspective, the stakes are even higher. Many countries offer low-cost or free access to higher education – but with a critical condition: proficiency in the country's language. Universities in countries such as Germany, Spain, and China do not center English. Instead, they require CALP-level proficiency in German, Spanish, or Mandarin, respectively. Without strong home language CALP, students are effectively shut out of these opportunities. Anderson (2011) highlights that in Latin America, learners who maintain and develop CALP in Spanish – alongside English – are far better positioned to access both local and global knowledge economies. Their dual proficiency enables them to pursue higher education either in English-speaking contexts or in their home countries, expanding their academic and professional horizons.

Furthermore, fostering home language CALP is not merely about preparing students for local success; it is about equipping them to participate in a globalised world where multilingualism is the norm, not the exception. As Acharya (2021) argues, multilingual awareness among educators is key to unlocking this potential. Teachers who value and integrate home languages into the classroom empower learners to navigate diverse linguistic landscapes. This opens pathways not just for academic success, but for employment and engagement in international contexts that demand high-level literacy in multiple languages.

Thus, the question is not whether we should support home language CALP – it is why we continue to ignore its critical role in favour of English-only approaches that serve limited futures. Elevating CALP in home and target languages simultaneously is not only pedagogically sound but globally strategic. It honours the full linguistic identity of the learner and positions them for success in any educational or professional context, whether local or international. Decolonising ELD begins with recognising this reality and centering the dual development of CALP as a matter of educational equity and opportunity.

## CALP development for diverse processing types

In the context of multilingual education, understanding how students process language is critical to supporting their growth in CALP. Not all learners engage with language in the same way, and traditional ELD programs often overlook this variability, resulting in instructional practices that serve some students while leaving others behind. A key factor in this dynamic is the distinction between GLPs and ALPs – two fundamentally different ways of acquiring and using language. Recognising these differences and designing instruction accordingly is essential to fostering equitable language development and ensuring that all learners have access to the tools needed for academic success.

GLPs thrive on patterns, contextual cues, and language that is meaningful in real-world settings. They often acquire language in chunks – phrases, scripts, or sentences – rather than through isolated vocabulary or explicit grammatical instruction. For these learners, language is not initially broken down into its component parts; instead, they process it holistically, making meaning through context and repetition. Tasks that rely heavily on rote memorisation or step-by-step deconstruction of language structures are often inaccessible to GLPs, as their processing style does not align with linear, rule-based instruction (Bhattacharya, 2007). In contrast, ALPs prefer structured environments that emphasise rules, sequences, and the breakdown of language into smaller, manageable units. They tend to excel in tasks that require analytic thinking, such as grammar drills, vocabulary quizzes, and stepwise language exercises.

In traditional ELD classrooms, the instructional design overwhelmingly favors ALPs. Teaching strategies commonly include isolated vocabulary lists, grammar worksheets, and linear writing tasks, all of which align with the strengths of analytic processors. While this approach may produce results for ALPs, it places GLPs at a distinct disadvantage. Without access to context-rich language, meaningful engagement, and the opportunity to process language in holistic ways, GLPs struggle to develop CALP effectively. Roessingh, Kover, and Watt (2005) highlight that CALP development is not simply about mastering academic vocabulary or grammatical structures; it requires deep engagement with language in meaningful contexts, where students can internalise complex ideas and apply them across disciplines.

The lack of differentiated instruction in ELD not only slows the CALP development of GLPs but often leads to misinterpretation of their abilities. Educators may perceive GLPs as disengaged or struggling due to perceived deficits, when the instructional methods do not align with their cognitive strengths. Mir and Khan (2022) note that language proficiency and processing are deeply interconnected, and when instruction does not support the cognitive-linguistic style of the learner, it results in diminished engagement and performance. In multilingual classrooms, this misalignment perpetuates inequity, as GLPs – often already navigating linguistic and cultural marginalisation – face additional barriers to academic language development.

To counter this, differentiated instruction must become the norm, not the exception. Teachers can support both processing types by incorporating varied instructional strategies that honour different pathways to language acquisition. For GLPs, this might include the use of storytelling, real-world problem-solving, project-based learning, and opportunities for oral language use in meaningful contexts. For ALPs, scaffolded grammar instruction, sentence deconstruction, and structured writing tasks remain valuable. Importantly, these approaches do not need to exist in silos. A well-designed ELD classroom can incorporate both, ensuring that all learners engage with language in ways that are accessible and empowering.

Additionally, integrating visual supports, graphic organisers, and student-created representations of knowledge can bridge the gap between these processing types. Bhattacharya (2007) found that visual representation of academic language – through drawing, diagrams, or charts – helps both GLPs and ALPs make sense of complex language structures, supporting their CALP growth across content areas. This type of holistic instruction not only supports diverse processing styles but also affirms students' identities by allowing them to demonstrate understanding in multiple ways.

The foundational work of Cummins (1981) reinforces the need for responsive and differentiated instruction in multilingual settings. His research underscores that CALP development is not uniform across learners and requires intentional scaffolding that aligns with students' linguistic backgrounds and cognitive styles. By designing ELD instruction that accommodates both GLPs and ALPs, educators can create equitable learning environments that foster deep, transferable academic language proficiency.

Ultimately, supporting CALP development for all students requires a shift in mindset. It calls for educators to move beyond one-size-fits-all instruction and towards pedagogies that recognise and value neurodiversity in language processing. When we design classrooms that affirm diverse ways of learning, we create space for all students – not just those who fit dominant models – to thrive academically. In doing so, we not only promote language proficiency but also educational equity.

## Strategies for holistic language instruction

In multilingual and neurodiverse classrooms, no single instructional method can meet the needs of all learners. Effective ELD must move beyond one-size-fits-all approaches and adopt strategies that support diverse language processing styles and linguistic backgrounds. This requires a holistic instructional design – one that integrates both chunk-based learning for GLPs) and rule-based scaffolding for ALPs, while also accommodating multiple home languages and dialects. By doing so, educators can create equitable and inclusive environments where all students can develop CALP in both English and their home languages.

### Designing for both GLPs and ALPs

Designing lessons that meet the needs of both GLPs and ALPs begins with recognising their distinct cognitive profiles. GLPs learn best through exposure to meaningful language chunks and contextual cues, while ALPs prefer structured, step-by-step breakdowns of language rules and patterns. A holistic instructional approach blends these methods, offering opportunities for all students to engage with language in ways that align with their strengths.

For example, in a science lesson about ecosystems, an educator might begin by introducing key academic phrases such as "energy transfer," "food chain," and "predator-prey relationship." These chunks offer GLPs meaningful, context-rich language that they can internalise through repetition and use in discussion or writing. At the same time, ALPs can work on deconstructing these phrases by examining word parts (prefixes, roots, and suffixes), identifying grammatical structures, and creating new sentences using similar patterns. This dual approach ensures that GLPs receive language input in manageable, meaningful units, while ALPs can analyze and apply language rules (Cenoz & Gorter, 2011).

Incorporating visual aids, sentence frames, and real-world examples further supports both processing types. GLPs benefit from hearing and seeing language used in context, while ALPs gain from dissecting and reconstructing the same language. This strategy is not about creating two separate lesson plans, but rather about designing flexible learning experiences that offer multiple pathways to academic language development.

## Accommodating multiple home languages and dialects

In diverse classrooms, students bring a variety of home languages and dialects, which can present challenges for educators – but also opportunities. A holistic approach recognises linguistic diversity as a strength and integrates it into instruction by focusing on universal academic concepts that transcend language boundaries. Concepts like cause and effect, sequencing, comparison, and classification are foundational to academic discourse and can be discussed in any language. Building lessons around these ideas allows students to engage meaningfully with content using their full linguistic repertoire (Duarte & Meij, 2018).

Multilingual glossaries translated academic materials, and student-led translations are valuable resources that support this approach. Providing students with key vocabulary and academic phrases in both English and their home languages not only reinforces CALP development but also validates students' linguistic identities. Where possible, educators can collaborate with students' families and community members to develop culturally and linguistically relevant resources. Safeer et al. (2024) emphasise the importance of leveraging community knowledge to bridge gaps in home language fluency, particularly when teachers themselves lack proficiency in the languages spoken by their students.

For instance, a teacher might assign a research project where students explore a scientific concept and present their findings using both English and their home language. Students can conduct research using multilingual resources, prepare visual presentations, and deliver oral reports in mixed-language formats. This not only strengthens CALP in both languages but also encourages students to see their home language as a valuable academic tool rather than something to be left at the classroom door.

## Facilitating CALP without teacher fluency

One of the most common concerns among educators in multilingual settings is how to support home language CALP when they do not speak those languages themselves. While this challenge is real, it is not insurmountable. Teachers can facilitate peer learning and group work where students are encouraged to use their home languages collaboratively. Small group discussions, partner work, and peer teaching allow students to process complex content in familiar linguistic terms before transitioning to

English. This approach aligns with holistic language development, allowing students to build understanding in their strongest language before expressing it in the target language (Brisk & Kaveh, 2019).

Multilingual multimedia resources, such as videos, educational apps, and articles in students' home languages, can serve as valuable models for academic language use. Teachers can curate or request recommendations from students and families to identify appropriate resources. These materials allow students to engage with academic content in their home language, providing a foundation upon which English CALP can be built.

Translation tools like Google Translate can also serve a purpose when used critically and cautiously. While such tools are not always accurate for complex or technical language, they can offer scaffolding for basic comprehension and vocabulary support. Teachers should encourage students to use translation tools as a starting point, followed by peer review and discussion to refine and clarify meaning. Safeer et al. (2024) note that while technology is no substitute for human interaction, it can be a useful aid when used thoughtfully and in combination with other strategies.

Moreover, educators can foster metalinguistic awareness by encouraging students to reflect on how language works in both English and their home languages. Activities that compare sentence structures, word meanings, or idiomatic expressions across languages help students develop a deeper understanding of linguistic patterns and promote CALP growth. Duarte and Meij (2018) advocate for this type of cross-linguistic transfer, emphasising that multilingual learners benefit from making explicit connections between languages.

## Creating equitable access through holistic instruction

Ultimately, holistic language instruction is about more than accommodating diversity – it is about equity. By designing lessons that support both GLPs and ALPs, integrating multiple home languages and dialects, and using available resources strategically, educators create classrooms where all students can develop the academic language skills they need to succeed. Cenoz and Gorter (2011) argue that multilingual education should not be confined to separate language silos but should reflect the integrated, dynamic ways in which students use language in their daily lives.

Holistic instruction affirms students' full linguistic identities and supports their growth in both English and home language CALP. It requires flexibility, creativity, and a commitment to viewing linguistic diversity as an asset rather than a barrier. When educators embrace this approach, they move closer to decolonising language education and ensuring that all learners can thrive academically, regardless of how they process language or which languages they speak.

# Classroom examples

Differentiated instruction is not a theoretical ideal – it is a practical necessity in multilingual, neurodiverse classrooms. Educators face the daily challenge of supporting students with diverse language processing styles and linguistic backgrounds, often within the same learning environment. The following case studies highlight how tailored instructional strategies can support both GLPs and ALPs while simultaneously promoting CALP in both English and home languages. These real-world examples demonstrate that inclusive, holistic instruction is both achievable and impactful.

## Case study 1: Supporting GLPs and ALPs in the same lesson

In a sixth-grade social studies classroom, students were learning about migration patterns and cultural diffusion. The teacher, aware of the diverse processing styles in the classroom, intentionally designed the lesson to accommodate both GLPs and ALPs. The core objective was for students to understand and explain key factors that influence migration, using academic language appropriate to the content area.

To support GLPs, the teacher introduced the concept using visuals and key phrases such as "push and pull factors," "economic opportunity," and "cultural integration." These phrases were provided as pre-written chunks on cards, which students used to create mind maps connecting causes and effects. Students worked in small groups to build visual timelines of migration events, labeling each event with a combination of provided language chunks and phrases in their home language.

ALPs, on the other hand, engaged in a more traditional task: reading a short informational text about migration patterns and writing a structured summary. They were guided to break down complex sentences, identify key vocabulary, and rephrase ideas in their own words. Grammar scaffolding was provided to support sentence construction, including verb tense review and transitions for cause-effect relationships.

Despite the differing tasks, both groups presented their work in a gallery walk, sharing their findings first in their home language, then in English. This approach allowed for cross-linguistic transfer, reinforcing CALP development in both languages. Students demonstrated not only content understanding but the ability to use academic language appropriate to social studies. As Kałdonek-Crnjaković and Płachta (2024) note, differentiated instruction that addresses diverse linguistic and cognitive needs fosters meaningful engagement and improved academic outcomes. In this case, GLPs benefited from contextual, chunk-based learning, while ALPs gained through structured analysis – both pathways leading to growth in CALP.

## Case study 2: Developing home language CALP across dialects

In a high school language arts class, students participated in a writing project centered on personal narratives. The teacher recognised that students spoke various dialects of Spanish, including Caribbean, Central American, and South American variants, each with distinct vocabulary and syntactic patterns. Rather than standardising the language of instruction, the teacher encouraged students to draft their essays in their home dialects, emphasising the value of linguistic authenticity.

The project began with a brainstorming session in students' home languages, followed by drafting essays that explored a significant life experience. Students worked individually or in pairs to draft, revise, and peer review their narratives entirely in their dialect. During revision, students identified key academic language and concepts – such as "resilience," "identity," and "conflict resolution" – and collaboratively translated these into academic English, discussing how the meaning might shift across languages and dialects.

This approach promoted flexibility and honoured linguistic diversity, while ensuring that students developed CALP in both languages. Abdelmoula, Samira, and Abdelmajid (2019) argue that allowing students to engage with academic tasks in their first language promotes deeper cognitive engagement and facilitates more effective transfer to English. In this case, students gained confidence in both their linguistic and academic identities. By affirming dialectical variation and supporting collaborative translation, the teacher empowered students to become active agents in their language development, enhancing both CALP and metalinguistic awareness.

## Case study 3: Preparing students for global opportunities

In an eleventh-grade ELD class, the teacher introduced a project-based learning unit titled "My Future, My Language," which asked students to research higher education opportunities in their home countries. The goal was to explore global pathways to university, with a focus on understanding the academic language required for admission and success in those settings.

Students selected a university in their country of origin – or a country where their home language is spoken – and researched entrance requirements, available programs, and language proficiency expectations. They gathered information using websites, brochures, and interviews (when possible) in their home languages. Students were tasked with identifying key academic terms used in the target university's language, translating them into English, and comparing how these terms are used in both contexts.

Throughout the unit, students created multilingual portfolios that included: a summary of university programs, a list of required academic terms in both languages, and a short reflection on how maintaining CALP in their home language could support their future academic goals. The culminating activity was a multimedia presentation delivered in both English and their home language, showcasing their findings.

This project served multiple purposes: it built students' awareness of educational opportunities beyond the U.S., reinforced the value of home language CALP, and provided authentic motivation to engage with academic language. Shareefa (2020) emphasises that differentiated, project-based learning supports multilingual learners by making content relevant and empowering. In this case, students not only strengthened their CALP in both languages but also gained a sense of purpose and direction for their academic futures. One student noted, "I didn't know I could go to university in my home country without perfect English. Now I want to keep learning both."

## Differentiated instruction in action

These case studies illustrate that supporting diverse learners does not require entirely separate lesson plans but thoughtful, inclusive design that values how students learn and what languages they bring with them. As Ankrum (2007) found in her research on exemplary teaching, differentiation is not just a strategy but a mindset – one that sees linguistic and cognitive diversity as assets rather than challenges.

In each case, students engaged with academic content through both English and their home languages, using processing styles that aligned with their strengths. Whether through visual mapping, collaborative translation, or project-based research, the goal remained the same: to develop CALP in ways that are meaningful, accessible, and empowering. By integrating differentiated instruction into daily practice, educators can support multilingual and neurodiverse learners in ways that prepare them not just for classroom success, but for a future of global opportunity.

# Extension activities

Holistic language instruction is most effective when it moves beyond theoretical understanding and into classroom practice. Educators and students alike benefit from hands-on, reflective activities that support multilingualism and diverse language processing styles. The following extension activities are designed to deepen educators' awareness of their instructional approaches and provide students with meaningful opportunities to apply CALP in both English and their home languages. These activities reflect the growing consensus in multilingual education that fostering academic literacy across languages and processing styles is essential for equity and inclusion (Goltsev & Bredthauer, 2020).

## For educators

Reflection: Audit and redesign for processing inclusivity

Begin by selecting a lesson from your current curriculum and critically examining it for processing bias. Does the lesson rely heavily on linear, rule-based instruction – favoring ALPs – or does it offer opportunities for GLPs to engage through context, patterns, and holistic learning? For example, consider whether students are asked to memorise vocabulary in isolation or if they are encouraged to use language chunks in meaningful ways.

After identifying any imbalances, redesign one element of the lesson to include GLP-friendly strategies. This might involve incorporating visual aids, sentence frames, or collaborative storytelling. Goltsev and Bredthauer (2020) emphasise that teacher preparation must include training on recognising and addressing diverse processing needs. By intentionally adapting lessons, educators promote more equitable access to academic content and support CALP growth for all students.

Activity: Home language and dialect mapping

Map the home languages and dialects represented in your classroom. This can be a simple list or a visual map showing linguistic diversity. Once this is complete, brainstorm ways to integrate these languages into academic instruction. For instance, could key terms be translated with student input? Can students share examples from their home language during discussions?

This mapping helps educators move from passive recognition of linguistic diversity to active inclusion. Panzarella and Sinibaldi (2018) advocate for collaborative translation and multilingual activities to validate student identities and deepen academic engagement. By involving students in the process, educators empower them as co-creators of knowledge and linguistic resources.

## For students

Bilingual academic posters

Ask students to create a bilingual academic poster on a topic relevant to the current unit of study. The poster should present information in both English and the student's home language, demonstrating CALP in both languages. Key requirements may include academic vocabulary, visual elements, and an oral presentation component delivered in both languages.

This activity supports translanguaging, fosters metalinguistic awareness, and affirms students' bilingual identities. Zahner, Calleros, and Pelaez (2021) found that multilingual expression in academic tasks enhances both comprehension and confidence. Additionally, this project allows students to draw upon their linguistic strengths while practicing content-specific communication in English.

University exploration project

Invite students to research a university in a country where their home language is spoken. The focus should be on academic language requirements: What proficiency levels are required? What types of academic writing or communication are expected? Students can present their findings in a report or presentation, using both English and their home language.

This project builds awareness of global academic pathways and reinforces the value of home language CALP. Kopečková and Poarch (2022) highlight that exploring pluralistic language frameworks in education prepares students for real-world multilingual contexts. By researching universities abroad, students recognise the importance of maintaining academic proficiency in their home language – not only for personal identity but also for future educational and career opportunities.

### Bridging practice and empowerment

These extension activities create a bridge between theory and practice, helping educators reflect on their instructional choices and giving students tangible opportunities to apply their linguistic assets. Through reflection, redesign, and student-led exploration, classrooms become spaces where linguistic diversity and varied processing styles are not only accommodated but celebrated. Ultimately, these activities contribute to the larger goal of decolonising language education – empowering all learners to develop CALP in ways that honour their full linguistic and cognitive identities.

## Looking ahead: Building a dual-language CALP ecosystem

Developing CALP is a complex and dynamic process that must account for both how students process language and the languages they bring with them. Throughout this chapter, we have explored how GLPs and ALPs require different yet complementary instructional approaches to succeed academically. We have also examined the necessity of supporting CALP not only in English but across all home languages and dialects, affirming that multilingualism is a strength, not a barrier. Building a dual-language CALP ecosystem – one that empowers students to develop academic proficiency in both their home language and English – is essential for educational equity, cognitive development, and future readiness in a global context.

A central takeaway is that CALP development is not uniform. GLPs thrive in environments where language is contextual, meaningful, and presented in patterns or chunks, while ALPs excel when instruction is structured, sequential, and rule-based. Holistic instruction that integrates both approaches ensures that no student is excluded from academic language growth due to a mismatch in processing style. When educators intentionally design lessons that offer multiple entry points – chunk-based resources for GLPs and analytic scaffolding for ALPs – they foster a classroom environment where all learners can thrive. These differentiated strategies not only support language acquisition but also affirm students' cognitive identities, contributing to greater engagement, retention, and long-term academic success.

Equally important is the role of home languages and dialects in CALP development. When instruction prioritises English at the expense of students' first languages, it not only undermines academic growth but perpetuates systemic inequities. A dual-language approach, by contrast, recognises that home language CALP is foundational – not supplemental – to success in English. Moreover, as discussed in this chapter, multilingual CALP opens doors to global educational and career opportunities, particularly in regions where university education is conducted in languages other than English. Holistic language instruction allows students to maintain and deepen their home language CALP even when their teacher lacks fluency in those languages, using strategies like peer learning, multilingual resources, and community engagement to bridge gaps in instructional capacity.

In this way, holistic instruction is a tool of equity. It removes the expectation that teachers must be fluent in every home language and instead empowers them to facilitate language development through collaborative and inclusive methods. It also ensures that students are not forced to choose between their linguistic identity and academic achievement. By creating space for translanguaging, student-led translation, and dual-language academic tasks, educators foster environments where all students are prepared not only for local academic success but for participation in a multilingual, interconnected world.

Looking ahead, these classroom-level strategies must be expanded into policy and systemic reforms if we are to create sustainable, equitable change. Chapter 5 will explore how to scale these approaches by examining the role of school and district policy, teacher preparation programs, and educational standards in either supporting or undermining dual-language CALP development. We will examine how to advocate for multilingual resources, institutional support for differentiated instruction, and the inclusion of home language CALP as a core component of academic assessment and success. Building a dual-language CALP ecosystem at scale requires more than individual effort – it demands systemic transformation that values linguistic and cognitive diversity as essential elements of a just and effective education system.

By embracing a holistic, dual-language approach to CALP development, we move closer to an educational model that truly serves all learners. The work begins in the classroom – but its impact must ripple outward, shaping the structures that govern how language education is delivered, valued, and resourced. Only then can we ensure that every student, regardless of processing style or linguistic background, can thrive.

# Summary

This chapter explored the imperative of decolonising ELD through the dual development of CALP in both home and target languages. By recognising the diverse language processing styles of Gestalt and Analytic Language Processors, we examined the limitations of one-size-fits-all instruction and the need for differentiated, holistic teaching practices. The chapter highlighted the global importance of home language CALP – not only for academic success but also for higher education and career opportunities beyond English-dominant contexts. Practical strategies were provided to support multilingual learners even when teachers lack proficiency in students' home languages, demonstrating that equity in language education is both achievable and essential. Ultimately, fostering CALP across languages affirms students' full linguistic and cognitive identities, equipping them to thrive in an interconnected, multilingual world.

## Key takeaways

- CALP development differs between GLPs and ALPs, requiring differentiated instruction tailored to each processing style.
- Holistic instructional strategies – such as storytelling, real-world tasks, and peer collaboration – support CALP for all learners across home and target languages.

- Home language CALP is foundational, not supplementary, to English CALP and supports long-term academic and cognitive growth.
- Teachers do not need fluency in all home languages to support CALP; multilingual resources, peer learning, and community engagement can bridge gaps.
- Multilingual CALP opens global opportunities, preparing students for higher education and employment in diverse linguistic contexts.
- Decolonising ELD means valuing linguistic diversity and rejecting English-only paradigms, ensuring equitable access to academic success.

Supporting CALP in both home and target languages is not a luxury – it is a necessity for equitable, inclusive education. By embracing holistic, context-rich instruction that honours neurodiversity and multilingualism, educators can dismantle assimilationist practices and build learning environments where all students are empowered to succeed. This work begins in the classroom, but its impact must extend to policy and systemic change – topics that will be explored in the next chapter as we examine how to scale dual-language CALP development across schools and districts.

# 5
# Policy and practice recommendations

## Learning objectives

- Understand how colonialism and global power structures have shaped ELD policies, contributing to systemic inequities for multilingual and neurodiverse learners.
- Examine current ELD practices across global, U.S., U.K., and Commonwealth contexts, identifying the tensions between English language acquisition and home language preservation.
- Explore policy gaps and innovations in language education, with a focus on strategies that promote linguistic diversity, neurodiversity, and cognitive justice.
- Analyse how plurilingual and inclusive language policies can support the development of CALP in both home and target languages.
- Reflect on the role of educators, communities, and policymakers in advancing equitable, multilingual education systems that move beyond English-only paradigms.

## Rationale

Educational equity for multilingual and neurodiverse learners cannot be achieved through classroom practice alone – it requires systemic transformation rooted in just and inclusive language policies. The persistence of English-dominant instruction across global, national, and regional contexts is not accidental; it reflects historical legacies of colonialism and current economic structures that privilege English at the expense of linguistic diversity. This chapter examines how ELD policies have been shaped by these forces and explores how they continue to marginalise learners whose linguistic and cognitive identities fall outside normative frameworks. By analyzing policy landscapes across global, U.S., U.K., and Commonwealth settings, this chapter aims to equip educators, advocates, and policymakers with the tools to critique current approaches and envision alternatives. Through comparative analysis, identification of policy gaps, and exploration of promising plurilingual and neurodiversity-affirming models, readers are invited to reimagine language education as a site of liberation rather than assimilation. True linguistic justice demands not only awareness but action – this chapter provides a foundation for both.

## Introduction: The need for systemic change

Throughout the preceding chapters, we have explored how ELD programs often reflect deficit-based frameworks that marginalise multilingual and neurodiverse learners. We have seen that traditional ELD instruction disproportionately favors ALPs while neglecting GLPs, and prioritises English monolingualism at the expense of home language development. These practices are not incidental – they are rooted in systemic ideologies that have historically privileged English as the dominant language in education, governance, and global discourse. Addressing these inequities requires more than classroom-level intervention; it demands systemic change at global, national, and local levels of policy and practice.

Language policy plays a central role in shaping educational equity. As Bianco (2010) argues, language policies are not merely administrative tools – they are powerful mechanisms that influence cultural diversity, social inclusion, and access to opportunity. In the absence of inclusive policies, multilingual and neurodiverse learners continue to navigate educational systems that are not designed to support their full linguistic and cognitive identities. This results in persistent disparities in academic achievement, social integration, and long-term outcomes.

The global dominance of English further compounds these challenges. As Crystal (2003) notes, English has become the lingua franca of international business, science, and technology. While this status affords certain benefits – such as facilitating cross-border communication – it also perpetuates linguistic hierarchies that privilege English speakers and marginalise speakers of other languages. In many educational systems, particularly at the K–12 level, English proficiency is treated as a prerequisite for academic and professional success, reinforcing systemic inequities and contributing to cultural erasure. That said, in higher education and some professional sectors, multilingualism is increasingly recognised as an asset – particularly when additional languages align with global markets or scholarly exchange. Yet even in these spaces, English typically retains primacy, and the value placed on other languages often depends on their perceived economic or geopolitical utility. The result is a global pressure to conform to English language norms – often at the expense of broader linguistic diversity and cognitive justice.

Given these realities, this chapter focuses on the urgent need for policy reform across multiple contexts. We will explore how ELD is implemented in global, U.S., U.K., and Commonwealth settings, examining the historical legacies and current practices that shape language education in each region. By identifying policy gaps and promising innovations, we aim to chart a path towards systemic change – one that supports dual-language CALP development, affirms linguistic and neurodiverse identities, and promotes equity at scale. True educational justice cannot be achieved without rethinking the policies that govern language instruction. This chapter invites readers to engage with this challenge and consider how policy transformation can foster more inclusive, effective, and liberatory language education systems worldwide.

## ELD in a global context

The global dominance of English did not arise by accident. Its spread is deeply intertwined with the history of colonialism, which positioned English as the language of power, administration, and control in colonised regions. Nowhere is this more evident than in India, where British colonial rule established English as the medium of governance and education. English functioned as a gatekeeping tool, granting access to economic and social mobility only to those who could master it (Pennycook, 1998).

This model was replicated throughout the British Empire, where English was deliberately imposed to standardise communication and facilitate colonial administration. As Chen (2018) notes, language colonialism was not simply about linguistic exchange – it was a deliberate strategy to consolidate imperial power, erode indigenous languages, and reshape cultural identities.

Today, English continues to dominate the global linguistic landscape, functioning as a lingua franca in business, academia, and technology. The perception of English as the language of upward mobility persists, reinforcing the notion that academic and professional success depends on English proficiency. This is evident in the prominence of international standardised tests such as the TOEFL and IELTS, which serve as gatekeepers to higher education and employment opportunities worldwide. While these assessments claim to measure readiness for global engagement, they often disadvantage multilingual learners by valuing standardised English over local linguistic competencies. Xu (2010) argues that the global status of English reinforces inequitable power dynamics, privileging English speakers while marginalising those whose academic strengths may lie in other languages.

This global dynamic presents a key tension for educators and policymakers: How can we prepare students to participate in a globalised world where English holds significant utility, without contributing to the erosion of cultural and linguistic diversity? There is no question that English proficiency can open doors – but this should not come at the cost of students' home languages and identities. The risk of cultural and linguistic erasure is particularly acute in contexts where English-only education policies are implemented without regard for students' linguistic backgrounds or processing styles. Monolingual instruction not only limits access to academic content for many learners but also perpetuates the colonial mindset that devalues non-English languages.

To address this, it is essential to develop policies that support bilingual or multilingual education systems, recognising the importance of home language CALP alongside English development. Plurilingual approaches, which value the dynamic use of multiple languages in educational settings, offer a promising alternative to the dominance of English-only instruction. These policies affirm linguistic diversity as a resource rather than a challenge and help create equitable learning environments that foster both local and global competencies.

Ultimately, while English will likely remain a key global language, its role in education must be reimagined to support linguistic equity and cultural preservation. Moving beyond English-only paradigms towards inclusive, multilingual education is not only a pedagogical imperative but a moral one – essential to dismantling the colonial legacies that continue to shape language education worldwide.

## ELD in the United States

ELD in the United States has long been shaped by assimilationist ideologies that prioritise English monolingualism and marginalise both Indigenous and immigrant languages. From the earliest days of public education, policies and practices sought to suppress linguistic diversity under the guise of national unity and social cohesion. Indigenous communities, in particular, were targeted through boarding school systems designed to "civilise"

Native children by stripping them of their languages and cultures. McCarty and Watahomigie (1998) highlight how these programs enforced linguistic assimilation through punitive measures, leading to significant language loss and cultural disconnection that persists today.

The 20th century saw continued efforts to subordinate home languages, particularly among immigrant populations. While pockets of bilingual education existed, the dominant narrative framed English acquisition as both a civic duty and a measure of individual worth. This context set the stage for the Bilingual Education Act of 1968, the first federal recognition of the educational needs of English learners. While the Act aimed to provide support for students with limited English proficiency, its implementation varied widely, and it often positioned bilingualism as a transitional phase towards full English assimilation rather than as an enduring asset. The Act's eventual repeal under No Child Left Behind (NCLB) in 2001 marked a significant regression. NCLB prioritised standardised testing and English-only instruction, effectively dismantling support for home language development and reinforcing deficit-based models of language learning (Bartolomé, 2006).

These shifts coincided with the rise of English-only movements, which gained traction in the late 20th century and significantly influenced ELD policies. Proponents of English-only legislation framed linguistic diversity as a threat to social cohesion and economic progress, advocating for laws that restricted the use of non-English languages in public settings, including schools. Bartolomé (2006) argues that these movements perpetuate colonial legacies by reinforcing the notion that English is the only legitimate language of instruction and public discourse, undermining linguistic equity and cultural preservation.

In recent years, however, a growing recognition of the value of bilingualism has led to a resurgence of dual-language immersion programs. These programs aim to develop proficiency in both English and a partner language, fostering bilingualism, biliteracy, and cross-cultural competence. Unlike transitional bilingual education, dual-language models affirm the long-term maintenance of home languages, positioning them as equal to English. Yet access to such programs remains uneven, with availability often limited to specific regions or communities with sufficient political and financial support. Additionally, the design of many dual-language programs still tends to favor analytic language processing, leaving GLPs without adequate support.

A significant challenge in the current landscape is the intersection of ELD and neurodiversity, particularly regarding standardised testing and rigid instructional frameworks. Most ELD assessments and curricula are designed for analytic processors, emphasising linear, decontextualised language tasks that disadvantage GLPs. Furthermore, neurodiverse students often face compounded challenges, as their language acquisition needs are often addressed through separate special education frameworks that fail to integrate multilingual supports. This disjointed approach results in inconsistent or inadequate services, especially in contexts where language and cognitive diversity intersect.

Policy gaps further exacerbate these challenges. ELD program funding varies widely by state, often reflecting broader inequities in public school funding. Some states provide robust support, while others allocate minimal resources, leaving educators without the tools needed to implement effective, inclusive instruction. Callahan et al. (2020) highlight how state-level policy variability creates significant disparities in immigrant student inclusion, with many systems failing to support home language development in meaningful ways. For Indigenous communities, the situation is even more dire. Despite the recognised importance of revitalising Indigenous languages, few public schools provide systematic support for this work, perpetuating historical patterns of linguistic suppression (McCarty & Watahomigie, 1998).

To move towards equity, federal and state policies must shift from an English-dominant model to one that fully supports multilingualism and neurodiversity. This includes restoring and expanding funding for dual-language programs, embedding home language development into ELD standards, and ensuring that instructional and assessment practices are accessible to all language processors. Without these reforms, ELD will continue to reinforce systemic inequities, failing to serve the very learners it is intended to support.

## ELD in the United Kingdom

The United Kingdom's approach to English language education cannot be separated from its colonial legacy. As a global imperial power, the UK established English as the language of governance, commerce, and education across its colonies. This was not simply a matter of linguistic preference – it was a deliberate policy of cultural domination. English was imposed through colonial education systems, often to the detriment of indigenous languages and knowledge systems. Spolsky (2021) notes that language was a key tool of imperial control, used to consolidate power and reshape the identities of colonised peoples. A striking example is found in colonial Hong Kong, where education policies prioritised English-medium instruction, marginalising Cantonese and creating a hierarchy of linguistic legitimacy (Sweeting & Vickers, 2006).

Domestically, post-war immigration to the UK from former colonies brought multilingualism into British schools. This influx of linguistic diversity prompted a shift in educational policy, from an assumption of English homogeneity to a need for accommodating students who spoke other languages. Initially, this took the form of compensatory education aimed at "integrating" immigrant children, often framed within an assimilationist paradigm. Over time, English as an Additional Language (EAL) programs emerged, designed to support students in acquiring English proficiency while participating in mainstream education.

Current EAL practices focus on language support for immigrant children, particularly those who arrive in the UK with limited English proficiency. While EAL services are intended to aid linguistic and academic integration, tensions persist around the balance between promoting English proficiency and maintaining students' home languages. In many cases, support for home language maintenance is minimal or absent, reflecting a broader societal ambivalence towards multilingualism. Gill (2022) argues that UK education law continues to grapple with the colonial context in which it was formed, often prioritising assimilation into English-speaking norms over genuine support for linguistic diversity.

These tensions manifest in practical and policy challenges. One major issue is the disparity in funding for EAL programs across different parts of the UK. While some local authorities prioritise EAL services and allocate sufficient resources, others provide limited or inconsistent support. This results in uneven experiences for multilingual learners, depending on their geographic location. Additionally, the UK's education policy is influenced by broader debates around multiculturalism versus assimilation. While the rhetoric of multiculturalism suggests a valuing of diversity, in practice, many schools emphasise English proficiency and social integration without systematically supporting students' cultural and linguistic identities.

Policy innovations aimed at supporting EAL learners have been sporadic and regionally variable. Some schools have developed robust language support models, including bilingual teaching assistants, culturally relevant curricula, and community engagement initiatives. However, without national-level mandates or sustained funding, such practices remain the exception rather than the rule. Moreover, standardised assessments and accountability measures often pressure schools to prioritise rapid English acquisition, sidelining long-term bilingualism or biliteracy goals.

As such, the UK's EAL landscape reflects both progress and persistent challenges. While there is recognition of the need to support multilingual learners, policies often fall short of affirming home languages as assets. The legacy of colonialism continues to shape attitudes towards language education, privileging English while leaving little space for systemic support of linguistic diversity. Addressing these issues requires more than incremental changes – it demands a critical reexamination of educational values and a commitment to building equitable, multilingual learning environments that truly reflect the diversity of the UK's student population.

## ELD in Commonwealth nations

Commonwealth nations share a common thread in their linguistic histories: the legacy of British colonial rule. Across regions as diverse as South Asia, Sub-Saharan Africa, and Oceania, English was systematically imposed through colonial education systems as both a tool of governance and a symbol of power. Matson (1993) describes how English, along with common law, was exported to colonies not merely for administrative convenience but as part of a broader project to reshape local societies along British lines. This linguistic imposition positioned English as the language of access – to education, economic opportunity, and legal recognition – while relegating indigenous languages to the private or informal spheres.

In the post-colonial era, many of these nations have retained English as an official language, reflecting its entrenched role in government, law, and higher education. However, English often functions as more than an administrative language; it is also a marker of social privilege. Crowley (1970) notes that in many Commonwealth countries, English proficiency is still equated with intelligence, modernity, and upward mobility, reinforcing socio-economic divides established during colonial rule. This dual role – as both official language and status symbol – complicates efforts to create equitable, multilingual education systems.

## Regional variations in ELD

In India, English occupies a unique position. With over a thousand languages spoken across the country, English is often used as a link language, facilitating communication across linguistic boundaries. However, this practical role is overshadowed by English's function as a marker of socio-economic status. Proficiency in English often determines access to elite education, employment, and social capital, reinforcing systemic inequalities. Masembe (2003) emphasises that in postcolonial societies like India, English-medium education is seen as a pathway to global opportunity, yet it often marginalises students from rural or non-English-speaking backgrounds. While India's constitution recognises multiple official languages, the dominance of English in academic and professional domains continues to perpetuate disparities in access and achievement.

In South Africa, the linguistic landscape is shaped by the legacy of apartheid and the country's commitment to recognising its myriad official languages. English, while not the most widely spoken first language, remains dominant in formal education and public life. The challenge lies in balancing English proficiency with the promotion and preservation of indigenous languages such as Zulu and Xhosa. Despite policy commitments to multilingual education, resource limitations and societal attitudes often hinder implementation. Masembe (2003) points to similar dynamics in other African nations, where English is privileged in education systems at the expense of local languages, despite official support for linguistic diversity.

In Australia, the impact of English on Indigenous communities is profound. English was imposed through colonisation, resulting in the suppression and, in many cases, extinction of Aboriginal languages. Education systems historically operated as instruments of assimilation, using English-only instruction to erase Indigenous linguistic and cultural identities. Today, there are growing efforts to reverse this damage through bilingual education and language revitalisation programs. However, significant challenges remain. Funding disparities, limited teacher training, and societal undervaluing of Aboriginal languages continue to impede progress. Crowley (1970) highlights how, in Australia and other settler-colonial contexts, the legacy of British language policy still influences contemporary attitudes and educational priorities.

## Innovative approaches

Despite these challenges, there are innovative efforts across Commonwealth nations to create more equitable, multilingual education systems. In India, some schools have implemented three-language formulas, incorporating local, regional, and English languages into instruction. These models aim to balance national unity with local identity, although implementation remains inconsistent. In South Africa, mother-tongue-based education initiatives have shown promise in early grades, supporting CALP development in students' first languages before transitioning to English. These programs align with global research indicating that strong home language foundations support better outcomes in second-language learning.

In Australia, language immersion programs in Aboriginal communities have helped revitalise endangered languages while promoting bilingual proficiency. Some schools have partnered with Indigenous elders and community members to integrate cultural knowledge and language into the curriculum, fostering a sense of belonging and identity among students. These case studies demonstrate that, when adequately supported, schools can serve as hubs for linguistic and cultural preservation, even within English-dominant systems.

These examples illustrate that post-colonial education systems are not bound to perpetuate colonial legacies. Through deliberate policy choices and community engagement, it is possible to build bilingual and multilingual education programs that honour both indigenous languages and the practical utility of English. Masembe (2003) concludes that while the legacies of colonial language policy remain strong, there is also significant potential for transformation – if education systems are willing to reimagine language instruction as a site of equity and empowerment rather than control.

## Policy implications across contexts

Across global education systems, a shared tension persists: the pressure to deliver English proficiency as a global skill while also preserving linguistic and cultural diversity. In each context explored – whether the United States, United Kingdom, or Commonwealth nations – ELD policies are shaped by histories of colonisation, economic globalisation, and social inequality. While the particulars differ, a global commonality emerges: current policies too often frame home languages as obstacles rather than assets, and favor English-only instruction as the default model of educational success.

The global dominance of English is undeniable, particularly in domains like business, academia, and technology. As Doiz, Lasagabaster, and Sierra (2011) note, the internationalisation of education has fueled a rapid expansion of English-medium instruction, often without adequate support for students' first languages. This shift is not neutral. It reinforces linguistic hierarchies that marginalise non-English speakers and undermines local and Indigenous languages. Moreover, it places undue cognitive and academic strain on multilingual learners – especially those who process language differently, such as GLPs.

To address these inequities, multilingual education policies must be reimagined. Grommes and Hu (2014) advocate for plurilingual models – approaches that view language competencies as interconnected and dynamic, rather than siloed. Plurilingual education affirms students' linguistic repertoires, integrating home languages into academic learning rather than relegating them to informal spaces. Such policies promote inclusion, cognitive flexibility, and deeper academic engagement. Crucially, they recognise that linguistic diversity and English proficiency are not mutually exclusive but mutually reinforcing when supported effectively.

## Policy recommendations by region

### United States

In the U.S., decades of "English-only" policies have created systemic barriers for multilingual learners. To move towards equity, renewed support for dual-language programs is essential – including investment in curriculum development, teacher training, and community engagement. Given the decentralised nature of U.S. educational governance – and the increasing erosion of federal oversight in some regions – this shift may not come uniformly from the federal level. However, states and districts, particularly in linguistically diverse areas, have the opportunity to lead in developing robust, inclusive language education policies.

Equally important is the promotion of translanguaging – a pedagogical approach that allows students to draw on all their languages during learning. Translanguaging supports both CALP and cognitive development, particularly for GLPs, by making academic content more accessible and meaningful.

To truly advance equity, state standards should explicitly include home language development as part of ELD goals, and assessment models must evolve to evaluate multilingual competencies, not just English proficiency. As Hornberger and Vaish (2009) argue, language policy in multilingual societies must prioritise additive bilingualism, where English is added to a strong foundation in the home language – rather than replacing it. While national policy may lag, local innovation offers a promising path forward.

## United Kingdom

The UK must address funding disparities in EAL programs and provide consistent, national-level support. Policy should mandate integration of home languages into the curriculum, including bilingual materials, assessments, and community language partnerships. This would shift EAL from a transitional support service to a foundational component of multilingual education.

Moreover, professional development for educators should include training on inclusive language pedagogies, including how to support GLPs and neurodiverse learners within EAL contexts. Grommes and Hu (2014) emphasise that inclusive language policy must be reflected in classroom practices, teacher education, and systemic accountability.

### Commonwealth Nations

In post-colonial contexts, particularly in nations like India, South Africa, and Australia, policy must elevate Indigenous and home languages to co-equal status with English. This involves legal protections for linguistic rights, investment in teacher training for bilingual education, and the development of culturally relevant curriculum resources. Hornberger and Vaish (2009) highlight the success of locally grounded multilingual policies that draw on community knowledge and support mother-tongue instruction alongside English.

Additionally, governments should monitor and assess the impact of English-medium instruction, ensuring it does not exacerbate socio-economic divides or displace local languages. Plurilingual policies that center local language needs and contexts offer a path towards more equitable and sustainable language education systems.

## Synthesis

Systemic transformation of language education requires more than classroom change – it demands policy reforms that affirm linguistic diversity, promote equitable access to English, and support all learners, including those with diverse processing styles. Whether in the U.S., UK, or Commonwealth nations, multilingual and inclusive policies are essential for dismantling the colonial legacies that persist in education. By embracing plurilingualism, supporting home language CALP, and designing systems that reflect linguistic justice, we can move towards educational models that truly serve all learners in a globalised world.

When I first began teaching in a district that branded itself as inclusive, I believed it. Our mission statements were translated. Our PDs cited equity. We had diversity committees and posters in multiple languages. But in the IEP room, I watched a child's first language reduced to a data point – something to be "accommodated" but not integrated. Their home tongue was framed as an obstacle, not a resource. I remember sitting quietly as the team debated whether a bilingual aide would "confuse" them. I kept thinking: Who are we afraid of confusing – the child, or the system?

Policy can't manufacture care. But it can remove the obstacles that keep care from taking root. It can open doors to belonging – or quietly close them under the weight of compliance. The work of transformation lives not just in the letter of the law, but in the spirit, we bring to interpreting it.

## Questions for reflection or discussion

- How do historical colonial structures continue to shape ELD policies in each context?

- o Consider the enduring influence of colonial education systems on current language policies. How do these legacies affect decisions about which languages are valued in schools, who has access to academic opportunities, and how language learning is framed?

- What can nations learn from one another in balancing English instruction with home language preservation?
  - o Reflect on the comparative approaches explored in this chapter. What successful strategies or policies from one region might inform or inspire reform in another? How can international collaboration support more equitable and multilingual education systems?
- How can multilingual and neurodiverse learners be better supported within existing frameworks?
  - o Think about the intersection of language processing differences and linguistic diversity. What changes are needed in curriculum, assessment, and teacher training to ensure that all learners – regardless of language background or processing style – can thrive academically and develop CALP in both English and their home languages?

These questions aim to prompt critical engagement with the systemic issues surrounding ELD. They invite educators, policymakers, and community members to imagine what linguistically just and inclusive education could look like – and to take steps towards making that vision a reality.

## Summary

This chapter explored the systemic roots of ELD policies and their lasting impact across global, U.S., U.K., and Commonwealth contexts. It examined how colonial legacies and English language dominance continue to marginalise home languages and neurodiverse learners, reinforcing educational inequities. By analyzing regional practices and highlighting policy gaps, the chapter presented a compelling case for plurilingual, inclusive approaches that affirm linguistic and cognitive diversity. Promising innovations – such as dual-language programs, translanguaging, and mother-tongue instruction – were presented as actionable alternatives to English-only paradigms. Ultimately, achieving equity in language education requires not only pedagogical shifts but also systemic policy reform that dismantles assimilationist models and positions multilingualism as a foundational asset for all learners.

## Key takeaways

- ELD policies globally reflect colonial legacies, privileging English and marginalising home languages through assimilationist models.
- Multilingual and neurodiverse learners are underserved by current systems, which favour analytic language processing and English monolingualism.
- Home language CALP development is essential for equitable academic outcomes and global competency, yet often neglected in policy frameworks.
- Plurilingual education models and translanguaging offer inclusive alternatives, supporting both linguistic equity and cognitive flexibility.
- Policy reform must include funding, teacher training, and curriculum support for home languages, while recognising diverse language processing styles.

- Cross-context collaboration and localised approaches are vital for reimagining ELD as a tool of empowerment rather than control.

Language education is not neutral – it is deeply political, shaped by histories of power, domination, and resistance. To move beyond the colonial legacies embedded in current ELD policies, educators, policymakers, and communities must advocate for systems that honour the full linguistic and cognitive identities of all learners. A truly just and inclusive language education system recognises multilingualism as a strength, not a challenge, and designs for diversity at every level – from classroom practice to national policy. The path forward requires courage, collaboration, and a shared commitment to linguistic justice.

# Conclusion: Reframing language education for equity and liberation

As we arrive at the conclusion of this work, it is important to pause and reflect not only on the ideas we've explored, but on the underlying systems and assumptions that brought us here. Language education, as it exists today, did not emerge in a vacuum. It is the product of deliberate historical choices – many of which were designed not to uplift, but to control; not to empower, but to assimilate. The central thesis of this book has been to challenge those colonial legacies embedded in ELD practices and to offer a vision of education that affirms the full linguistic and neurological identities of all learners.

This is not simply a call for reform in curriculum or instruction. It is a call to fundamentally reframe our understanding of language, identity, and power. For too long, the dominant narrative in ELD has positioned English as the sole gateway to academic and social success, marginalising home languages and the diverse ways in which language is processed and acquired. This approach has particularly failed multilingual and neurodiverse learners, especially GLPs, whose needs are routinely overlooked by systems designed for conformity, not inclusion.

Throughout this book, we have examined how current practices in ELD perpetuate inequities and explored how educators, policymakers, and communities can disrupt these patterns. What follows is a brief recap of the key insights from each chapter – each one building towards a vision of linguistic justice grounded in critical pedagogy, Natural Language Acquisition, and the PTMF. These insights serve not as a checklist, but as guideposts – markers to help navigate the ongoing work of decolonising language education, in both thought and practice.

## Chapter recap

**Chapter 1** examined the colonial origins of ELD, revealing how TESOL frameworks continue to function as tools of linguistic assimilation. Grounded in a deficit mindset, these models position English as the measure of success, requiring students to shed their home languages to access education, employment, and social mobility. By tracing the lineage of ELD to colonial policies of language suppression – where indigenous and minority languages were forcibly replaced – the chapter challenged the notion that English dominance is neutral or natural. Instead, it argued for a shift towards TEFL-informed approaches, where English is treated as a contextual skill rather than a replacement language, thereby honouring multilingualism as a strength, not a problem to be fixed.

**Chapter 2** explored how the suppression of home language in ELD classrooms impacts learners at the most personal level – through the erosion of identity, belonging, and intergenerational connection. Language is not just a tool; it is the vessel of culture, family, and self. When students are forced to abandon their first / home language, the result is often alienation – from their heritage, from their families, and from themselves. Through case studies, this chapter illustrated the psychological and academic costs of English-only models and called for classroom practices that actively integrate and uplift home languages. In doing so, it reframed language maintenance not as a luxury, but as a necessity for student well-being and success.

**Chapter 3** focused on a group rarely acknowledged in language education: Gestalt Language Processors. These learners process language holistically, acquiring phrases and scripts before breaking them into flexible, meaningful parts. Traditional ELD instruction, with its linear, rule-based focus on individual words and grammar, is not designed for GLPs – and yet they are often misunderstood, marginalised, or pathologised within these systems. This chapter made the case for context-rich, TEFL-inspired instruction that aligns with GLP needs, integrating strategies like storytelling, role-play, and translanguaging. Recognising GLPs not as deficient but as different is essential to creating an inclusive, equitable learning environment for all students.

**Chapter 4** turned to the development of Cognitive Academic Language Proficiency, a critical component of academic success that cannot thrive without deliberate, sustained support in both home and target languages. This chapter outlined how CALP development varies between GLPs and Analytic Language Processors, and how instructional strategies must be differentiated accordingly. It offered holistic, adaptable methods for supporting CALP – even when teachers are not fluent in their students' home languages – highlighting the global importance of maintaining home language CALP for higher education and career opportunities. In reframing CALP as a dual-language goal, this chapter challenged the dominance of English-only models and provided actionable tools for inclusive practice.

**Chapter 5** expanded the conversation beyond the classroom, examining the policy landscape that shapes and constrains ELD practice. It highlighted how language policy – rooted in colonialism and maintained through global power structures – continues to marginalise linguistic and neurodiverse identities. Through analysis of policy gaps and emerging innovations in plurilingual education, this chapter called for systemic change: from funding priorities and assessment reform to the inclusion of neurodiversity in policy design. True linguistic justice, it argued, cannot be achieved through classroom strategies alone – it requires collective action to reimagine and reconstruct the systems that govern language education, ensuring they serve all learners, not just those who conform to the dominant model.

Taken together, these chapters offer a comprehensive framework for reimagining language education – one that challenges colonial legacies, centers linguistic and cognitive diversity, and places equity and liberation at the heart of ELD practice. The recurring themes of home language validation, neurodiversity inclusion, and contextualised, culturally responsive pedagogy reveal that true educational transformation cannot be achieved through minor adjustments to existing systems. Instead, it requires a paradigm shift – a commitment to dismantling the structures that have long marginalised multilingual and neurodiverse learners, and to building new models that honour the full humanity of every student. As we turn to the path ahead, the question is no longer whether change is necessary, but rather how we will choose to enact it – within our classrooms, institutions, and communities.

## A call to action: Reclaiming language education for justice

Decolonising language education is not a theoretical exercise – it is a practical, urgent, and ongoing commitment. The work outlined in this book must now be translated into action, sustained not just by individuals, but by communities, institutions, and systems. It begins with a shift in mindset – from viewing English as the default or superior language, to recognising and affirming the rich linguistic and cognitive diversity that students bring into educational spaces. Below are key steps for different stakeholders – each interconnected, each essential to creating liberatory learning environments that serve all students.

### For educators

In the classroom, change begins with intentional practice. Integrate translanguaging into your daily instruction, allowing students to draw on their full linguistic repertoire as they make meaning and engage with content. Use context-rich, real-world scenarios to support GLPs and ALPs alike, ensuring that instruction is not only accessible, but also relevant and empowering. Adopt differentiated strategies that account for diverse processing styles, moving beyond rigid, one-size-fits-all models. Above all, challenge English-only assumptions – both in your pedagogy and within your school culture. Advocate for curriculum and policies that uplift home languages, making it clear that linguistic diversity is not a problem to solve, but a strength to celebrate.

## For administrators and policymakers

Systemic change requires resource allocation and structural support. Fund and expand dual-language programs that promote CALP development in both home and target languages. Ensure that ELD curricula are inclusive by design, accounting for neurodiverse learners, particularly GLPs, whose needs are often overlooked. Reform assessment policies to accommodate diverse ways of processing and expressing language and provide professional development that equips educators to serve multilingual, neurodiverse populations effectively. Policies must move beyond rhetoric and deliver tangible support – from classroom resources to equitable staffing and program evaluation.

## For communities

Language does not live only in schools – it lives in families, neighborhoods, and cultural spaces. Honour and revitalise home languages by creating spaces where they can thrive. Engage in storytelling, intergenerational dialogue, and cultural practices that center your linguistic heritage. Advocate for your schools to recognise families as linguistic and cultural partners, not passive recipients of educational decisions. Community engagement is not peripheral to language education – it is at its core. When families and communities are valued, students are empowered to bring their whole selves into the learning space.

## For researchers and advocates

Research shapes policy, informs practice, and defines legitimacy. It is time to move away from deficit-based models that reduce learners to a set of deficiencies. Promote Able Grounded Phenomenology (AGP) (Kupferstein, 2020) and critical pedagogy as foundations for ethical, relevant research that centers the lived experiences of autistic, neurodiverse, and multilingual learners. Challenge the dominance of standardised assessments as sole measures of success, and advocate for inclusive methodologies that honour the complexity of language and identity. In teacher training, prioritise critical consciousness, ensuring that new educators are equipped not just with strategies, but with a deep understanding of power, privilege, and resistance in language education.

While each of these spheres – classroom practice, policy reform, community engagement, and research – holds distinct responsibilities, they are deeply interconnected. Transforming language education requires coordinated effort across all levels, rooted in a shared commitment to equity, inclusion, and liberation. No single action will suffice; rather, it is through sustained, collective movement that we dismantle colonial narratives and replace them with models that affirm every learner's linguistic and cognitive identity. As you reflect on your role in this work – whether as an educator, policymaker, advocate, or community member – consider how your daily choices can either reinforce or resist the systems we have critiqued. The following reflection activities are offered as a space to begin that process of personal and collective reckoning, and to envision the practical steps that can carry this work forward.

# Reflection activities: From awareness to action

Decolonising language education begins within systems, but it also begins within ourselves. The work of transformation is both external and internal – requiring not only shifts in policy and practice, but shifts in perspective, intention, and accountability. Reflection is not a passive act; it is a critical tool for identifying complicity in oppressive systems and imagining new, liberatory pathways forward. The following activities are designed to support ongoing personal and collective growth, inviting you to interrogate your relationship with language, power, and pedagogy. Whether undertaken individually or in a group, these reflections aim to bridge the gap between theory and practice, cultivating critical consciousness and purposeful action in service of multilingual and neurodiverse learners.

## Activity 1: Reflecting on your linguistic identity

Consider your own relationship with language. What languages do you speak, understand, or have encountered in your life? How have these shaped your educational experiences, access to opportunities, and sense of self? Reflect on the privileges or challenges you have faced because of your linguistic background. For educators and policymakers, ask: how might your linguistic identity inform your decisions, biases, or assumptions in your professional role? Write a personal narrative or engage in dialogue with peers to explore how your language journey impacts your approach to multilingualism, neurodiversity, and power in education.

## Activity 2: Auditing language practices

Conduct a classroom, school, or institutional audit with a focus on language use and policies. Identify where colonial assumptions persist – such as English-only mandates, devaluation of home languages, or standardised assessments that ignore processing diversity. Consider the hidden curriculum: what messages are students receiving about which languages are valued or marginalised? Document examples and reflect on how these practices impact multilingual and neurodiverse learners. Finally, identify actionable changes – whether small shifts in classroom language norms or larger institutional reforms – that could begin to disrupt these patterns and create more inclusive, affirming environments.

## Activity 3: Developing an action plan

Select one strategy or idea from this book that resonated with you. It could be integrating translanguaging, designing context-rich instruction for GLPs, or advocating for dual-language CALP development. Develop a practical action plan to implement this in your context. Outline the specific steps you will take, the resources or support you will need, and anticipate potential challenges or resistance. Consider how you will measure progress and sustain this change over time. If working in a group, collaborate to develop shared goals and strategies for accountability.

## Activity 4: Advocacy in action

Choose a specific policy or institutional change that would meaningfully support multilingual and neurodiverse learners in your context. Write a letter to a policymaker, administrator, or leadership team outlining the issue, the evidence supporting change (drawing from this book or local data), and clear recommendations for action. Use this letter as both an advocacy tool and a reflection on your role as a change agent. Consider sharing it publicly, as part of a campaign, or within a professional network to amplify the call for systemic reform.

## Closing

These activities are not endpoints – they are starting points for deeper engagement with the work of liberating language education from its colonial constraints. Through reflection, dialogue, and action, we begin to cultivate praxis – the integration of theory and practice in pursuit of justice. The goal is not perfection, but progress rooted in critical awareness and collective care. By engaging with these reflections honestly and intentionally, you become part of a growing movement to create educational spaces where all learners – multilingual, neurodiverse, and marginalised – are not only included but empowered. Let these reflections guide your next steps and may those steps ripple outward into transformation that endures.

## Final reflection: Language as liberation, poetry as home

As a youth, I often felt like a stranger adrift in a world I was never meant to inhabit. I could see the rhythms of the dominant culture – its expectations, its language, its carefully laid paths – but I could not find my place within them (Hoerricks, 2024e). Words floated past me, inaccessible and alien. I was functionally illiterate when I graduated from a prestigious American high school, a fact that left me carrying a silent weight of shame for years. I had survived school, but I had not belonged to it, nor it to me (Hoerricks, 2024d). For someone like me – an autistic GLP – the education system's insistence on linear language acquisition was a daily dissonance, reinforcing the message that the way I learned was wrong, that I was wrong (Hoerricks, 2024a).

For much of my early life, language was a force of exile, a symbol of my disconnect from the dominant culture that surrounded me. I could not write, not in any meaningful sense, and reading brought little joy – only confusion and fatigue. I lived, as I wrote in The Last Person Before Gender, on the margins of language, desperately seeking a foothold in a world that felt constructed to deny my existence (Hoerricks, 2024b). It was not until my late 30s, through immense effort and a stroke of good fortune in finding a mentor who understood me, that I finally gained functional literacy. And with it came something I had never known: a depth of experience, of connection, of being that words alone cannot fully convey. Language ceased to be a prison; it became a door flung open to a landscape I could finally explore.

This transformation brought with it the most unexpected and enduring joy: poetry. As I shared in Poetry as Therapy: Expat from Vaerensland (Hoerricks, 2024e), I now write not to impress, but to exist more fully – to map the contours of my mind and to offer others a glimpse of the worlds I inhabit. Poetry, with its rhythm and gestalt, fits me in ways conventional prose never did. It is language in motion, in pattern, in context – everything that GLPs like me need to thrive. Writing has become my quiet rebellion, a means to process, to heal, and to connect with others who have felt the sting of alienation and the yearning for a place to call home.

I write this book as an expat in multiple senses – an outsider to the dominant culture, an outsider to the conventional language systems of the neuro-majority, and an outsider who has found their way back to the center, not by conforming, but by rewriting the terms of engagement. My work in a Title 1 school in Los Angeles has shown me that I am not alone – that many learners, especially those who are multilingual and neurodiverse, face the same structural barriers that kept me silent for so long. It is for them – and for the child I once was – that I write, that I teach, that I advocate.

Language can wound, but it can also heal. It can exclude, or it can make space for those long pushed to the margins. We who have been shaped by systems that sought to erase us have the power to reshape those systems, to transform education from a tool of assimilation into a space of belonging, empowerment, and justice (Hoerricks, 2024c). This is our collective responsibility – to build classrooms and communities where every learner's voice is heard, honoured, and nurtured. For me, writing is both refuge and revolution, and in sharing this with you, I hope you find inspiration to join in this quiet, joyful rebellion – one where language becomes not a barrier, but a bridge.

# Appendix: Resources for educators – Tools for decolonising ELD practice

## Foundational readings

Curated texts to build critical consciousness around language, identity, power, and pedagogy.

- Freire, P. (1970). Pedagogy of the Oppressed.
  - o Grounding text in critical pedagogy; essential for understanding the power dynamics in education.
- Paris, D., & Alim, H. S. (2017). Culturally Sustaining Pedagogies: Teaching and Learning for Justice in a Changing World.
  - o Offers frameworks for culturally and linguistically responsive teaching.
- Blanc, T., Blackwell, L., & Elias, N. (2023). Natural Language Acquisition for Autistic GLPs.
  - o Practical and theoretical guide on NLA, specific to GLPs.
- Kupferstein, H., Chau, V., & Watts, C. A. (2023). Autistic Consumer Audit of UC Davis MIND Institute's Mutant Angelman Mice and Their Translational Value Toward the Human Autistic Experience.

  - Model of research that applies Able Grounded Phenomenology in critiquing traditional autism research.

## Practical tools and guides

Resources that provide ready-to-use strategies and implementation support for educators.

- Translanguaging classroom resources (CUNY-NYSIEB):
  - Downloadable lesson plans, classroom posters, and guides for integrating translanguaging.
  - https://www.cuny-nysieb.org
- GLP communication and literacy supports:
  - Visual supports, scripting strategies, and multimodal tools designed for GLPs.
  - Recommendations: *Meaningful Speech* platform (www.meaningfulspeech.com), *AAC Language Lab, PrAACtical AAC blog*.
- Classroom language audit checklist (developed from Chapter 2):
  - Tool for identifying where home languages are excluded, devalued, or tokenised.
- This audit tool is intended as a flexible framework that educators can develop and adapt for their own classroom or school contexts. It may be created individually, guided by self-reflection, or developed collaboratively with students, families, and community members to ensure it reflects the lived experiences and linguistic realities of those it serves. The tool supports critical examination of where home languages are excluded, devalued, or tokenised, focusing on classroom environment, instructional practices, and school policies. It encourages educators to reflect on current practices

and identify concrete steps to foster linguistic inclusion and equity, grounded in meaningful engagement with their learning communities.

  - o Prompts for reflection and concrete action steps.

- In what ways are students encouraged – or discouraged – to use their home languages in my classroom, and how does this impact their sense of belonging?
- What assumptions do I hold about the role of English and home languages in academic success, and how do these assumptions shape my teaching?
- How can I create space for students and families to share their linguistic and cultural knowledge as co-creators of the learning environment?
- What is one specific change I can make this week to better support home language use or visibility in my classroom?
- Differentiated CALP activities:
  - o Dual-language CALP templates: storytelling prompts, visual organisers, and sentence starters for GLPs and ALPs.
- Educators can leverage Large Language Models (LLMs) to efficiently generate dual-language CALP supports such as storytelling prompts, visual organisers, and sentence starters tailored for both GLPs and ALPs. LLMs offer a practical and time-saving way to create differentiated materials, especially when teachers are not fluent in their students' home languages. However, it is important to note that LLMs are predictive tools, not translators – they generate responses based on patterns in data rather than true linguistic understanding. This means that translations produced by LLMs may lack accuracy, cultural nuance, or context-specific meaning, and should always

be reviewed by native speakers or community members when possible. Used thoughtfully, LLMs can be valuable aids in scaffolding CALP, but they should complement – not replace – human insight and collaboration in multilingual education.

- Prompt: Please translate this high school mathematics lesson on logarithms into Mexican Spanish as spoken in Oaxaca, ensuring that the math terminology is appropriate for secondary education students in that region. Use clear, student-friendly language and maintain cultural relevance where possible. Do not use overly formal or Spain-specific phrasing. After translating, highlight any terms that may need review by a local speaker for accuracy and nuance.
- Prompt: Translate this logarithms lesson into standard Salvadoran Spanish suitable for secondary school students in El Salvador. Use regionally appropriate vocabulary and avoid Spain-specific terms. Ensure the mathematical terminology is correct for educational use in El Salvador, and keep the tone accessible and engaging for teenagers. Flag any terms that might benefit from clarification by a native speaker for educational use.
- Prompt: Please translate this lesson on logarithms into Mandarin Chinese using Simplified Chinese characters appropriate for secondary school students in Mainland China. Ensure that all math terminology aligns with standard educational usage in China and that the explanation style matches instructional norms for Chinese classrooms. Keep the tone clear and concise. Note any terms that should be checked for regional clarity or accuracy.

# Policy and advocacy resources

For educators engaging in systemic change beyond the classroom.

- WIDA guiding principles of language development (Reimagined with a decolonial lens).
  - Use WIDA as a starting point, while critically evaluating its alignment with your context.
- Local and national language rights organizations:
  - E.g., Center for Applied Linguistics, TESOL International's Advocacy Center (with caveats for TESOL's colonial underpinnings).
  - Form local alliances with parent advocacy groups for bilingual and special education rights.

# Reflective practice and community building

Spaces and tools to foster ongoing learning and connection.

- Professional learning communities (PLCs):
  - Guide for forming a PLC focused on decolonising ELD.
- PLCs offer a powerful way for educators to engage in collaborative, sustained inquiry focused on decolonising ELD practices. This guide supports the formation of PLCs that center linguistic equity, neurodiversity, and critical pedagogy, providing frameworks for setting shared goals, facilitating reflective dialogue, and examining classroom practices through an anti-colonial lens. Whether school-based or virtual, these PLCs foster collective accountability and growth, encouraging educators to challenge systemic assumptions, share strategies, and co-create inclusive,

liberatory learning environments for multilingual and neurodiverse students.
    - o Sample reflection questions and meeting prompts.
- How do our current ELD practices reflect or resist colonial assumptions about language and learning?
- In what ways are home languages visible, valued, or marginalised in our classrooms and school policies?
- What barriers do neurodiverse, multilingual students face in our context, and how can we address them collaboratively?
- What is one change we can implement this month to make our instruction more inclusive and affirming of linguistic and cognitive diversity?
- Recommended podcasts and media:
    - o The AutSide by Jaime Hoerricks (AutSide.Substack.com).
    - o Decolonial Thought & Praxis (JairoFunez.Substack.com).
- Writing prompts for educator reflection:
    - o "When have I silenced a student's language, knowingly or unknowingly?"
    - o "How can I make space for different ways of processing and expressing language?"

## Suggested further reading: Beyond ELD

Expand educators' understanding of intersectionality, neurodiversity, and systemic oppression.

- Erevelles, N. (2011). Disability and Difference in Global Contexts: Enabling a Transformative Body Politic.

- Lhamon, C. E. (2021). Dear Colleague Letter on Supporting Neurodiverse Learners in K–12 Settings. U.S. Department of Education.
- Smith, L. T. (2012). Decolonising Methodologies: Research and Indigenous Peoples.

# Bibliography

Abdelmoula, E., Samira, R., & Abdelmajid, B. (2019). A case study of differentiated instruction in the EFL reading classroom in one high school in Morocco. *International Journal of English Literature and Social Sciences*.

Acharya, R. (2021). Using learners' home languages in English classrooms: Multilingual awareness of teachers. *Interdisciplinary Research in Education*, 6(2),107–116

Acharya, R. (2022). Using learners' home languages in English classrooms: Multilingual awareness of teachers. *International Journal of Multilingual Education*, 9(1), 54–68.

Alshihry, M. A. (2024). Heritage language maintenance among immigrant youth: Factors influencing proficiency and identity. *Journal of Language Teaching and Research*, 15(1), 112–125.

Anderson, C. E. (2011). CLIL for CALP in the multilingual, pluricultural, globalized knowledge society: Experiences and backgrounds to L2 English usage among Latin American L1 Spanish-users. *Latin American Journal of Content and Language Integrated Learning*, 4(2), 51–66.

Andrews, G., Prozesky, M., & Fouché, I. (2020). The multiliteracies learning environment as decolonial nexus: Designing for decolonial teaching in a literacies course at a South African university. *Scrutiny2*, 25(1), 64–85.

Ankrum, J. W. (2007). *Differentiated reading instruction in one exemplary teacher's classroom: A case study.*

Anuyahong, B., & Songakul, K. (2024). Analyzing the effectiveness of content-based language teaching (CBLT) approaches in integrating language learning with subject matter instruction in TEFL contexts. *International Journal of Advanced Research*.

Arnautović, L. (2022). TEFL versus TESOL: A comparative analysis of English instruction in non-native contexts. *Language Education Perspectives*, 8(1), 44–59.

Baker, W., Panero, S. M., Valencia, J. A. Á., Alhasnawi, S., Boonsuk, Y., Hoang Ngo, P. L., … & Ronzón-Montiel, G. J. (2024). *Decolonizing English in higher education: Global Englishes and TESOL as opportunities or barriers*. TESOL Quarterly.

Bamgbose, A. (1991). *Language and the nation: The language question in Sub-Saharan Africa*. Edinburgh University Press.

Bartolomé, L. (2006). Borderlands and the colonial legacy of "English only". *Human Architecture: Journal of the Sociology of Self-Knowledge*, 4(1), 5–27.

Bearse, C., & de Jong, E. J. (2008). Cultural and linguistic investment: Adolescents in a secondary two-way immersion program. *Equity & Excellence in Education*, 41(3), 325–340.

Bhattacharya, A. (2007). Student drawing and academic language processing. *Academic Exchange Quarterly*, 11(2), 82–89.

Bianco, J. L. (2010). The importance of language policies and multilingualism for cultural diversity. *International Social Science Journal*, 61, 37–67.

Blackledge, A. (1993). *Language, literacy, and education: A reader*. Multilingual Matters.

Blanc, M., Blackwell, A., & Elias, P. (2023). *Using the natural language acquisition protocol to support gestalt language development. Perspectives of the ASHA Special Interest Groups*.

Borelli, J., Silvestre, V. P. V., & Pessoa, R. R. (2020). Towards a decolonial language teacher education. *DELTA: Documentação de Estudos em Lingüística Teórica e Aplicada*, 36(3), 301–324.

Brisk, M., & Kaveh, Y. M. (2019). *Teacher education for bi/multilingual students*. Oxford Research Encyclopedia of Education.

Burchell, K., Jones, T., & Singh, R. (2024). Reassessing ELD frameworks: Beyond assimilation and toward equity. *International Journal of Language and Identity*, 9(1), 34–52.

Caddy, S. (2015). *Exploring strategies for teaching reading to English First Additional Language learners in Grade 2*. Reading Strategies Research.

Callahan, R. M., Gautsch, L., Hopkins, M., & Unda, M. D. C. (2020). Equity and state immigrant inclusivity: English learner education in ESSA. *Educational Policy*, 36(6), 1011–1053.

Canagarajah, S. (1999). *Resisting linguistic imperialism in English teaching*. Oxford University Press.

Cenoz, J., & Gorter, D. (2011). A holistic approach to multilingual education: Introduction. *The Modern Language Journal*, 95(3), 339–343.

Cheatham, G. A., Jiménez-Silva, M., & Park, H. (2015). Teacher feedback to support oral language learning for young dual language learners. *Early Child Development and Care*, 185(9), 1452–1463.

Chen, B. (2018). Study on colonialism of English and Spanish language. *International Journal of Language and Linguistics*, 5.

Christoun, L., & Wang, J. (2018). *Misconceptions about ELLs: Culturally responsive practices for general education teachers*. Culturally Responsive Education Studies.

Crowley, D. (1970). Emergent Commonwealth – I. *British colonial policy*. Unpublished Manuscript.

Crystal, D. (2003). *English as a global language*. Cambridge University Press.

Cummins, J. (1980). The cross-lingual dimensions of language proficiency: Implications for bilingual education and the optimal age issue. *TESOL Quarterly*, 14(2), 175–187.

Cummins, J. (1981). Empirical and theoretical underpinnings of bilingual education. *Journal of Education*, 163(1), 16–29.

Daly, N., & Sharma, S. (2018). Language-as-resource: Language strategies used by New Zealand teachers working in an international multilingual setting. *Australian Journal of Teacher Education*, 43(12), 35–50.

Daud, R. (2024). The cognitive benefits of speaking multiple languages. *European Journal of Linguistics*, 16(2), 88–97.

Dhami, N. (2024). Decolonizing language in education policies of Nepal. *Far Western Review*.

Doiz, A., Lasagabaster, D., & Sierra, J. (2011). Internationalisation, multilingualism and English-medium instruction. *World Englishes*, 30, 345–359.

Domke, L. M., May, L. A., Cerrato, M. A., Sanders, E. H., Kung, M., & Bingham, G. E. (2024). How dual language bilingual education preservice teachers draw upon and develop students' sociocultural competence. *Foreign Language Annals*, 57(3), 797–817.

Dorner, L. (2015). From global jobs to safe spaces: The diverse discourses that sell multilingual schooling in the USA. *Current Issues in Language Planning*, 16(2), 114–131.

Duarte, J., & Meij, M. G. D. (2018). A holistic model for multilingualism in education. *EuroAmerican Journal of Applied Linguistics and Languages*.

Duarte, J., & Meij, M. G. D. (2020). 'We Learn Together' – Translanguaging within a holistic approach towards multilingualism in education. *Inklusion und Bildung in Migrationsgesellschaften*.

Dube, T. (2020). Language, resistance and multilingualism in post-colonial Zimbabwe: The Kalanga and their struggle for recognition. *Journal of Southern African Studies*, 46(6), 1183–1201.

Ellis, R. (2005). *Instructed second language acquisition: A literature review*. Report to the Ministry of Education, New Zealand.

Friedenberg, J. E. (2002). The linguistic inaccessibility of U.S. higher education and the inherent inequity of U.S. IEPs: An argument for multilingual higher education. *Bilingual Research Journal*, 26(2), 309–326.

García, O., & Kleyn, T. (2016). *Translanguaging with multilingual students: Learning from classroom moments*. Routledge.

García, O., & Wei, L. (2014). *Translanguaging: Language, bilingualism and education*. Palgrave Macmillan.

García-Ponce, E. E. (2020). Influence of discrimination in the field of TESOL: Perspectives of Mexican EFL teachers. *GIST – Education and Learning Research Journal*.

Garza, T. O. D. L., Lavigne, A. L., & Si, S. (2020). Culturally responsive teaching through the lens of dual language education: Intersections and opportunities. *Universal Journal of Educational Research*, 8, 1557–1571.

Gelir, I. (2022). Technology-assisted language learning for neurodiverse learners. *Journal of Educational Technology Integration*, 11(2), 33–48.

Gill, A. (2022). *Comprehending the colonial context: Education and law*. Unpublished Manuscript.

Goltsev, E., & Bredthauer, S. (2020). Preparing teachers to foster multilingual literacy. In *Handbook of research on cultivating literacy in diverse and multilingual classrooms* (pp. 516–534). igi Global.

Graven, M., & Robertson, S. A. (2020). A mathematics teacher's response to a dilemma: 'I'm supposed to teach them in English but they don't understand'. *South African Journal of Childhood Education*, 10(1), 1–11.

Gray, M. (1998). Don't forget the home language: Creating a community of learners in second language classrooms. *Primary Voices K-6*, 6(4), 10–14.

Grommes, P., & Hu, A. (2014). *Plurilingual education: Policies-practices-language development*. John Benjamins.

Guo, Z., & Feng, Q. (2024). *An Ethnographic Case Study: Exploring an Adult ESL Learner's BICS and CALP Proficiency Disparity*. In Forum for Linguistic Studies (Vol. 6, No. 4, pp. 215–230).

Gupta, R. (2019). Teaching for diverse language processors: Inclusive strategies for EFL classrooms. *Journal of Inclusive Education*, 5(3), 142–155.

He, S., Yang, L., Leung, G., Zhou, Q., Tong, R., & Uchikoshi, Y. (2021). Language proficiency and competence: Upper elementary students in a dual-language bilingual education program. *Journal of Multilingual and Multicultural Development*, 43, 502–517.

Heffington, D. S., & Coady, M. R. (2022). Using visual supports to scaffold language and content learning for ELLs. *TESOL Journal*, 13(4), e00317.

Hoerricks, J. (2023). *No Place for Autism? Exploring the Solitary Forager Hypothesis of Autism in Light of Place Identity*. Lived Places Publishing.

Hoerricks, J. (2024). *Holistic Language Instruction. Addressing Literacy in Standard and Non-Standard Populations*. Lived Places Publishing.

Hoerricks, J. (2024a). *From panic to poetry: Finding my voice*. AutSide. https://autside.substack.com/p/from-panic-to-poetry-finding-my-voice

Hoerricks, J. (2024b). The last person before gender: The trauma of being unnamed. AutSide. https://autside.substack.com/p/the-last-person-before-gender-the

Hoerricks, J. (2024c). *The colonial blind spots in multilingual education*. AutSide. https://autside.substack.com/p/the-colonial-blind-spots-in-multilingual

Hoerricks, J. (2024d). *The lexicographer and the fae: Decoding the language of the in-between.* AutSide. https://autside.substack.com/p/the-lexicographer-and-the-fae-decoding

Hoerricks, J. (2024e). *Poetry as therapy: Expat from Vaerensland.* AutSide. https://autside.substack.com/p/poetry-as-therapy-expat-from-vrensland

Hornberger, N., & Vaish, V. (2009). Multilingual language policy and school linguistic practice: Globalisation and English-language teaching in India, Singapore, and South Africa. *Compare: A Journal of Comparative and International Education*, 39(3), 305–320.

Housel, D. A. (2021). Sophie's Choices: One TESOL Professional's Journey. *MEXTESOL Journal*, 45(4), n4.

Howard, K. B., Katsos, N., & Gibson, J. (2020). Practitioners' perspectives and experiences of supporting bilingual pupils on the autism spectrum in two linguistically different educational settings. *British Educational Research Journal*, 46(2), 292–311.

Jayasinghe, D. (2021). Colonial language suppression and educational inequity in South Asia. *Postcolonial Studies in Education*, 15(2), 87–104.

Jeganathan, K., & Shanmugam, M. (2022). Inclusive language instruction in multilingual classrooms: Pedagogical perspectives. *Journal of Language Teaching Research*, 7(3), 101–115.

Johnson, A. (2024). Dual language education and academic growth. *Teachers College Record*, 126, 183–213.

Jong, E., & Howard, E. R. (2009). Integration in two-way immersion education: Equalizing linguistic benefits for all students. *International Journal of Bilingual Education and Bilingualism*, 12(1), 81–99.

Joubert, M., & Sibanda, B. (2022). Whose language is it anyway? Students' sense of belonging and role of English for higher education in the multilingual South African context. *South African Journal of Higher Education*, 36(2), 55–70.

Kalati, E., & Memari, M. (2017). Differentiated instruction in multilingual classrooms: A review of pedagogical practices. *International Journal of Educational Development*, 9(2), 55–69.

Kałdonek-Crnjaković, A., & Płachta, K. (2024). *Differentiating for multilingual students' needs in a psychology classroom with English as a medium of instruction*. Applied Linguistics Papers.

Kamhi-Stein, L. D., Lee, I., & Johnson, A. (2021). Contextualising English: The TEFL-TESOL divide and its implications for multilingual learners. *TESOL Journal*, 12(3), 256–270.

Kani, Z. G., & Igsen, H. (2022). Bilingual English teachers' perspectives on "English-Only" policies in an EFL setting. *Educational Policy Analysis and Strategic Research*, 17(1), 127–141.

Kaveh, Y. M. (2020). Unspoken dialogues between educational and family language policies: Language policy beyond legislations. *Linguistics and Education*, 60, 100876.

Kazmi, S. S. (2022). The politics of linguistic marginalization in the third space: A postcolonial analysis. *Pakistan Journal of Social Research*.

Keiko, I. (2008). Young learners' gestalt and analytic strategy and the acquisition of chunks. *Language Studies*, 56, 189–214.

Kopečková, R., & Poarch, G. J. (2022). Learning to teach english in the multilingual classroom utilizing the framework of reference for pluralistic approaches to languages and cultures. *Languages*, 7(3), 168.

Kupferstein, H. (2020). *Able Grounded Phenomenology (AGP): Toward an ethical and humane model for non-autistic researchers conducting autism research* (Doctoral dissertation, Saybrook University).

Küppers, A. (2022). (Foreign) language education and its impact on equal opportunity and sustainability: A case study of a bilingual German-Turkish program. *Dilbilim Dergisi / The Journal of Linguistics*, 38, 67–85.

Lake, V. E., & Beisly, A. H. (2019). Translation apps: Increasing communication with dual language learners. *Early Childhood Education Journal*, 47(4), 489–496.

Lam, V. L., & Catto, A. C. (2023). Heritage language use and proficiency: Acculturation, identities, and psychological health. *Journal of Home Language Research*, 5(1), 22–39.

Li, X. (2022). *Envisioning TESOL through a translanguaging lens: global perspectives.* Edited by Zhongfeng Tian, Laila Aghai, Peter Sayer, and Jamie L. Schissel, Cham, Springer, 2020, 374 pp., ISBN: 978-3-030-47030-2, ISBN: 978-3-030-47031-9 (eBook).

Linse, C. (2013). Linguistic capital pays dividends: Treating Spanish as a valuable asset, not a problem. *Phi Delta Kappan*, 94(6), 32–35.

Lopriore, L. (2023). Gestalt language processors and foreign language education: Insights for teachers. *ELT Journal*, 77(1), 45–56.

Machaba, F., Sipholi, K., & Motseki, P. (2024). Multilingual students' solution strategies in solving linear programming problems: A case of national curriculum vocational level 3 mathematics students. *Journal of Culture and Values in Education.*

Magsalin, C. N. (2023). Community language learning in tertiary-level teachers. *Asian Journal of Education and Social Studies*, 42(2), 1–11.

Mak, E., Mauer, E., Luo, R., Zhou, Q., & Uchikoshi, Y. (2024). Cognitive demand in parent–child shared book reading and home language development among dual language learners. *International Journal of Bilingualism*, 28(1), 75–93.

Mak, E., Vanni, N. N., Yang, X., Lara, M., Zhou, Q., & Uchikoshi, Y. (2023). Parental perceptions of bilingualism and home language vocabulary. *Frontiers in Psychology,* 14, Article 1167123.

Martínez-Álvarez, P., & Chiang, H. M. (2020). A bilingual special education teacher preparation program in New York City: Case studies of teacher candidates' student teaching experiences. *Equity & Excellence in Education*, 53(2), 196–215.

Masembe, C. (2003). *Institutionalisation, perspectives, challenges, and pedagogical dimensions of the English language in the education systems of former British colonies in Africa: The case of Uganda, Kenya, and Zimbabwe*. Unpublished Manuscript.

Mason, R. J., Alvarez, P., & Chang, L. (2024). Language policy in practice: Examining TESOL's reach in U.S. schools. *Language Policy Review*, 17(1), 12–30.

Mataka, T. W., Bhila, T., & Mukurunge, T. (2020). Language in education policy: A barrier to academic and cognitive development of learners across grades. *South African Journal of Education*, 40(2), 117–124.

Matson, J. (1993). The common law abroad: English and indigenous laws in the British Commonwealth. *International and Comparative Law Quarterly*, 42, 753–779.

May, S. (2014). *The multilingual turn: Implications for SLA, TESOL and bilingual education*. Routledge.

McCabe, P. P., Timmons, M., & Heron, K. (2013). Meeting the needs of diverse learners: Differentiating instruction with menus for ELLs. *Intervention in School and Clinic*, 49(1), 22–29.

McCarty, T., & Watahomigie, L. (1998). Indigenous community-based language education in the USA. *Language Culture and Curriculum*, 11(3), 309–324.

McIntyre, E., & Kyle, D. W. (2008). *Effective literacy instruction for English learners: What teachers need to know*. Guilford Press.

McKinney, C. (2022). Coloniality of language and pretextual gaps: A case study of emergent bilingual children's writing in a South African school and a call for ukuzilanda. *Journal of Multilingual and Multicultural Development*, 45(6), 663–679.

Mezzadri, M. (2022). From 1960 to the present day: The influence of the gestalt theory on didactic devices for language teaching. *Language Teaching and Learning Review*, 11(2).

Mir, F. A., & Khan, A. (2022). The role of proficiency in Kashmiri language in phonological processing skills: A cognitive-linguistic approach. *East European Journal of Psycholinguistics*.

Mitits, L., Alexiou, T., & Milton, J. (2018). Does the language you speak at home affect the size of your L2 vocabulary? *The Language Learning Journal*, 46, 569–582.

Molyneux, P., Scull, J., & Aliani, R. (2016). Bilingual education in a community language: Lessons from a longitudinal study. *Language and Education*, 30(4), 337–360.

Monsores, J., Almeida, T., Quadros, L. C., & Quadros, J. R. (2020). Technology and gestaltism: A robotic-based learning aid tool. *IEEE Latin America Transactions*, 18, 1441–1447.

Mutongoza, B., Mutanho, C., Linake, M. A., & Makeleni, S. (2023). Reflections on decolonising medium of instruction at South African universities. *Research in Educational Policy and Management*.

Nagy, W., & Townsend, D. (2012). Words as tools: Learning academic vocabulary as language acquisition. *Reading Research Quarterly*, 47(1), 91–108.

Ngidi, S., & Mncwango, E. M. (2022). University students' perspectives on an English-only language policy in higher education. *The Journal for Transdisciplinary Research in Southern Africa*.

Nikitorowicz, J. (2012). Native language as a core value which creates the cross-cultural identity. *Family Upbringing*, 13(2), 59–72.

Nurshatayeva, A., & Page, L. C. (2019). Effects of the shift to English-only instruction on college outcomes: Evidence from Central Asia. *Journal of Research on Educational Effectiveness*, 13(2), 120–192.

O'Connor, M., O'Connor, E., Tarasuik, J., Gray, S., Kvalsvig, A., & Goldfeld, S. (2018). Academic outcomes of multilingual children in Australia. *International Journal of Speech-Language Pathology*, 20(4), 393–405.

O'Milligan, L. (2022). Decoloniality, language and literacy: Conversations with teacher educators. *Critical Studies in Teaching and Learning*, 10(2).

Orosco, M. J., & Abdulrahim, N. A. (2017). Culturally responsive evidence-based practices with English language learners with learning disabilities: A qualitative case study. *Educational Research Journal*, 1, 27–45.

Pacheco, M., David, S. S., & Jiménez, R. T. (2015). Translating pedagogies: Leveraging students' heritage languages in the literacy classroom. *Middle Grades Research Journal*, 10, 49–63.

Panzarella, G., & Sinibaldi, C. (2018). Translation in the language classroom: Multilingualism, diversity, collaboration. EuroAmerican Journal of Applied Linguistics and Languages, 5(2), 62–75.

Papapostolou, A., Manoli, P., & Mouti, A. (2020). Challenges and needs in the context of formal language education to refugee children and adolescents in Greece. *Journal of Education*, 9, 7–22.

Parajuli, B. (2021). Role of language in shaping cultural identity. *Marsyangdi Journal*, 2(1), 12–21.

Paterson, K. (2020). Using home language as a pedagogical resource: Working collaboratively with Ontario educators to support English language learners in the classroom. *Journal of the Canadian Association for Curriculum Studies*, 18, 93–94.

Pennycook, A. (1994). *The cultural politics of English as an international language*. Longman.

Pennycook, A. (1998). *English and the discourses of colonialism*. Routledge.

Percovich, A., Tosi, A., Chiruzzo, L., & Rosá, A. (2019, November). Ludic applications for language teaching support using natural language processing. In 2019 38th International Conference of the Chilean Computer Science Society (SCCC) (pp. 1–7). IEEE.

Perez Peguero, L. (2024). The impact of technology-enhanced language learning on bilingual education. *International Journal of Scientific Research and Management*, 12(3), 101–110.

Pila, O., & Mavuru, L. (2022). Natural sciences teachers' perceived cognitive academic language proficiency (CALP) needs. *Education and New Developments 2022 – Volume I.*

Puustinen, M., Baker, M., & Lund, K. (2006). GESTALT: A framework for redesign of educational software. *Journal of Computer Assisted Learning*, 22(1), 34–46.

Roessingh, H., Kover, P., & Watt, D. L. E. (2005). Developing cognitive academic language proficiency: The journey. *TESL Canada Journal*, 23(1), 1–27.

Rovira, L. C. (2008). The relationship between language and identity: The use of the home language as a human right of the immigrant. *Linguistic Rights Review*, 10(1), 55–70.

Ryan, È. (2021). The impact of home literacy on bilingual vocabulary development. *Bilingual Research Journal*, 44, 108–123.

Safeer, N., Hussain, I., Azhar, B., Shaikh, M. H., & Jakhrani, M. H. (2024). Challenges and strategies in teaching English in multilingual classrooms. *Journal of Policy Research*.

Santamaría, L. J. (2009). Culturally responsive differentiated instruction: Narrowing gaps between best pedagogical practices benefiting all learners. *Teachers College Record*, 111, 214–247.

Schecter, S., & Bayley, R. (1997). Language socialization practices and cultural identity: Case studies of Mexican-descent families in California and Texas. *TESOL Quarterly*, 31(3), 513–541.

Serafini, E. J., Rozell, N., & Winsler, A. (2020). Academic and English language outcomes for DLLs as a function of school bilingual education model: The role of two-way immersion and home language support. *International Journal of Bilingual Education and Bilingualism*, 25(5), 552–570.

Shareefa, M. (2020). Using differentiated instruction in multigrade classes: A case of a small school. *Asia Pacific Journal of Education*, 41, 167–181.

Simarmata, N. B. (2024). *Active learning strategies in teaching English as a foreign language*. Educational Innovations.

Skutnabb-Kangas, T. (2000). *Linguistic genocide in education – or worldwide diversity and human rights?* Routledge.

Smitherman, G. (2000). *Talkin and testifyin: The language of Black America*. Wayne State University Press.

Solis, E. N., & Flores-Chang, N. G. (2024). Preparing teacher candidates with pedagogical approaches for ELLs in hybrid/virtual learning spaces. *The CATESOL Journal*.

Soltero-González, L. (2009). Preschool Latino immigrant children: Using the home language as a resource for literacy learning. *Theory Into Practice*, 48(4), 283–289.

Spolsky, B. (2021). Imperialism and colonialism. In *Rethinking language policy*. Edinburgh University Press.

Swain, M., & Lapkin, S. (2005). The evolving sociopolitical context of immersion education in Canada: Some implications for program development. *International Journal of Applied Linguistics*, 15(2), 169–186.

Swanson, L. H., & Swanson, T. (2014). Literacy instruction for diverse learners: Research-based best practices. *Education Digest*, 80(1), 36–43.

Sweeting, A., & Vickers, E. (2006). Language and the history of colonial education: The case of Hong Kong. *Modern Asian Studies*, 41(1–40).

Tomaš, Z., Farrelly, R., & Haslam, M. (2020). *Meeting the needs of multilingual learners: A guide for educators*. TESOL Press.

Tong, V. M. (1996). Home language literacy and the acculturation of recent Chinese immigrant students. *Bilingual Research Journal*, 20(4), 523–543.

Torres-Velásquez, D., & Lobo, G. (2004). Culturally responsive mathematics teaching and English language learners. *Teaching Children Mathematics*, 11, 249.

Van Laere, E., & Braak, J. (2014). What role does the home language play in science achievement? *Journal of Multilingual Education*, 5(1), 21–38.

Wang, Z. (2018). *Evaluations of immersion teaching strategies in TEFL*. Advances in Social Science, Education and Humanities Research.

Xu, B. (2010). English as a global language: Its formation and consequences. *Foreign Language and Literature*.

Yang, J., & Jang, I. (2020). The everyday politics of English-only policy in an EFL language school: Practices, ideologies, and identities of Korean bilingual teachers. *International Journal of Bilingual Education and Bilingualism*, 25(6), 1088–1100.

Zahner, W., Calleros, E. D., & Pelaez, K. (2021). Designing learning environments to promote academic literacy in mathematics in multilingual secondary mathematics classrooms. *ZDM – Mathematics Education*, 53, 359–373.

Zano, K., & Baloyi, M. (2019). Complementing home languages and English first additional language through non-academic activities. *Children*, 9(1), 1–8.

Zhang, X., & Jiang, L. (2024). Enhancing dual language learners' language learning through parent–teacher partnerships. *Language Teaching Research*, 28(2), 189–210.

Zhang, X., & Jiang, L. (2024). *Enhancing dual language learners' language learning through parent–teacher partnerships*. Language Teaching Research.

# Glossary of key terms

**Academic Language:** Language used in formal educational contexts, including discipline-specific vocabulary, complex sentence structures, and language for reasoning and argumentation (Cummins, 1981).

**Analytic Language Processor (ALP):** A learner who processes language through linear, rule-based instruction, preferring explicit grammar, syntax, and vocabulary teaching (Bhattacharya, 2007).

**Assimilationist Education:** An educational model aimed at integrating students into the dominant culture by prioritising English and devaluing home languages. Often rooted in colonial and imperial ideologies (Bartolomé, 2006).

**Basic Interpersonal Communicative Skills (BICS):** Conversational language used in everyday social interactions. Typically develops in 1–2 years but does not reflect academic readiness (Cummins, 1981).

**Bilingual Education Act (1968):** The first U.S. federal law supporting bilingual instruction. Repealed under "No Child Left Behind" (2001), which prioritized English-only models (Callahan et al., 2020).

**Cognitive Academic Language Proficiency (CALP):** Proficiency in academic language needed for success in school, including abstract reasoning and discipline-specific vocabulary. Strong home language CALP supports English CALP (Cummins, 1981; Roessingh et al., 2005).

**Colonial Education:** Education systems used during colonization to promote English and suppress local languages and knowledge systems (Sweeting & Vickers, 2006; Spolsky, 2021).

**Culturally Sustaining Pedagogy:** Teaching that supports students in sustaining and growing their cultural and linguistic identities within the classroom (Paris & Alim, 2017).

**Critical Pedagogy:** An educational approach that challenges societal inequalities and centers learners' experiences and agency (Freire, 1970; Bartolomé, 2006).

**Decolonial Theory:** A critique of colonial legacies in knowledge, power, and education. Advocates for centering Indigenous and marginalised epistemologies (Gill, 2022; Spolsky, 2021).

**Differentiated Instruction:** Instruction designed to meet diverse learning needs, including varying language processing styles, cultural backgrounds, and neurodiversity (Ankrum, 2007; Safeer et al., 2024).

**Dual-Language Program:** An educational model that teaches in both English and a partner language to promote bilingualism, biliteracy, and academic achievement (Grommes & Hu, 2014).

**English as an Additional Language (EAL):** UK term for English language instruction for students who speak another language at home. Often used in immigrant integration programs (Gill, 2022).

**English Language Development (ELD):** Instructional programs focused on English acquisition, particularly for multilingual learners. Historically rooted in assimilationist frameworks (Bartolomé, 2006; Callahan et al., 2020).

**English-Only Movement:** Political and educational advocacy for English as the sole language of instruction and public discourse, often excluding other languages (Bartolomé, 2006).

**Equity in Education:** Ensuring fair access, opportunity, and outcomes for all learners, regardless of linguistic, cultural, or neurodiverse backgrounds (Callahan et al., 2020).

**Gestalt Language Processor (GLP):** A learner who acquires language through patterns, scripts, and chunks rather than isolated vocabulary or grammar rules. Benefits from context-rich, holistic instruction (Bhattacharya, 2007).

**Global English:** English as a global lingua franca used in business, academia, and international communication, often reinforcing linguistic hierarchies (Crystal, 2003; Doiz et al., 2011).

**Home Language:** The language(s) a student uses at home or in their community. Critical for identity development and academic success (Acharya, 2021).

**IELTS / TOEFL:** International standardised English proficiency tests often required for academic and professional access. Serve as linguistic gatekeepers (Doiz et al., 2011).

**Indigenous Languages:** Languages native to specific regions, often marginalised by colonial and post-colonial education systems (McCarty & Watahomigie, 1998).

**Language Justice:** The right of individuals and communities to access services, education, and civic participation in their home languages (Hornberger & Vaish, 2009).

**Multilingualism:** The use and support of multiple languages in education and society. Viewed as an asset in plurilingual education models (Grommes & Hu, 2014).

**Multimodal Learning:** Instruction that integrates visual, auditory, kinesthetic, and other sensory modes to support diverse learners, including GLPs and neurodiverse students (Bhattacharya, 2007).

**Natural Language Acquisition (NLA):** Developmental model that aligns with GLP needs by focusing on meaningful, context-rich language exposure rather than explicit instruction (Bhattacharya, 2007).

**Neurodiversity:** The natural variation in cognitive processing, including language acquisition. Encompasses learners who process language differently, such as GLPs and autistic students (Safeer et al., 2024).

**No Child Left Behind (2001):** U.S. federal education law that emphasised standardised testing and English proficiency, leading to reduced support for bilingual education (Callahan et al., 2020).

**Plurilingualism:** The dynamic use of multiple languages depending on context. Recognises the interdependence of linguistic skills (Grommes & Hu, 2014).

**Scaffolding:** Instructional supports provided to help learners access and master complex content. Gradually removed as independence increases (Roessingh et al., 2005).

**Standardised Testing:** Assessments designed to measure proficiency, often privileging dominant languages and processing styles, disadvantaging multilingual and neurodiverse learners (Zahner et al., 2021).

**TESOL / TEFL:** Teaching English to Speakers of Other Languages / as a Foreign Language. Often criticised for promoting English dominance and assimilation (Masembe, 2003).

**Translanguaging:** The fluid use of multiple languages by learners to make meaning and engage with content. Supports both CALP development and identity (Acharya, 2021; Grommes & Hu, 2014).

# Index

www.ingramcontent.com/pod-product-compliance
Lightning Source LLC
LaVergne TN
LVHW020045110826
845155LV00029B/634
*9781917503938*